The World of

RAYMOND
CHANDLER

The World of
RAYMOND CHANDLER

Edited by Miriam Gross

Introduction by Patricia Highsmith

A & W Publishers, Inc
New York

Contents

Illustrations

ILLUSTRATIONS

between pages 150 and 151

A moustachioed Marlowe in *The Brasher Doubloon*
Marlowe talks things over with LA cops
Marlowe accompanies Moose Malloy
Dick Powell in *Murder, My Sweet*
Humphrey Bogart in *The Big Sleep*
Robert Montgomery in *The Lady in the Lake*
George Montgomery in *The Brasher Doubloon*
Van Hefflin, the American radio Marlowe
Gerald Mohr, Marlowe on the radio
Philip Carey in the TV series *Philip Marlowe*
James Garner in *Marlowe*
Elliott Gould in *The Long Goodbye*
Robert Mitchum in *Farewell, My Lovely*
Claire Trevor as Velma/Mrs Grayle
Lauren Bacall as Vivien Reagan
Martha Vickers as Carmen Sternwood
Audrey Totter as Adrienne Fromsett
Nancy Guild as Merle Davis
Gayle Hunnicutt as Mavis Weld
Nina Van Pallandt as Eileen Wade
Charlotte Rampling as Velma/Mrs Grayle
Veronica Lake as Joyce Harwood
Barbara Stanwyck as Phyllis Dietrichson

Preface

MIRIAM GROSS

Raymond Chandler was approaching middle-age before he found his voice as a writer; he only wrote seven full-length books and basically they were all variations on the formula which he perfected in the first of them. *The Big Sleep.* Yet his impact has been deeper than that of any of his obvious competitors and his appeal has gone well beyond conventional crime-fiction addicts. If anything, it has increased in recent years – his novels have survived the phase of seeming dated and his achievement looks all the more intriguing now that it can be seen in historical perspective.

The essays in this book are primarily attempts to explore and explain that achievement. Although they include a number of memoirs, the main emphasis is on Chandler's writing rather than his life – partly because a substantial biography has recently appeared (and another is now being written), and partly because he represents an extreme case of the split between outward circumstance and inner fantasy. That split is, of course, one of the themes which any writer on Chandler must consider.

There were plenty of other paradoxes in Chandler: the mixture of toughness and sentimentality, for instance; the anti-literary stance which coexisted with intense literary ambition; initially he seemed a ruthlessly modern writer, with his mastery of the hard-boiled idiom, his big-city, underworld backgrounds, the streamlining which made him such a natural for Hollywood. It took longer to see the underlying romanticism or the debt to his English public school upbringing. And if he is a moralist, his morality seems at odds with his relish for violence.

All the contributors to this collection, not least those who knew him personally, deal in some measure with Chandler's inconsistencies. All of them agree that, as a writer, he owes everything to his style; which is perhaps just another way of saying that he *was* a writer, not just an entertainer, and one whose work seems likely to outlast many a contemporary with apparently more serious pretensions.

Introduction

PATRICIA HIGHSMITH

In a 1952 Penguin edition of *The Lady in the Lake* Elizabeth Bowen is quoted inside the back cover:

> Raymond Chandler is not just one more detective writer – he is a craftsman so brilliant, he has an imagination so wholly original, that no consideration of modern American literature ought, I think, to exclude him.

High praise. And in the same Penguin in regard to the first publication in England of 'Trouble is My Business', here is part of the blurb:

> The author tells his readers all they need to know, by relating only the action and the conversation. He does not stop to explain what his characters are thinking or to analyse their motives, but simply rushes them through a series of events . . .

Maybe that was news in those days. Writers have copied Chandler's style since. What was a new style, or attitude, in the 1940s has now become an ideal, or has at least set a fashion. But what writer has quite the same style as:

> 'I don't like your manner.'
> 'That's all right. I'm not selling it.'
> He reeled back as if I had hung a week-old mackerel under his nose.

Style is the man, but curiously Chandler's style does not much jibe with his character or his life. Or is he fooling the public all of the time? Or was he downright unhappy all of his life? Or what was he aiming at, as a writer? One of the strange facts about Chandler is that he wasn't a writer, not a fiction writer anyway, until his early forties. He was born in American of American Quaker and Irish parents, educated in England from early boyhood, because his abandoned mother returned there, and then he came back to America at twenty-four. After some wanderings, he ended in Los Angeles, that most soulless of American cities, and became an executive in an oil firm for a while. He married a woman named Cissy, eighteen years older than himself. He did *want* to write, as do many people who, for the most part, never make their mark or even get published. Another strange thing about Chandler is that when he eventually did start writing he did not make use of the formidable emotional material at his disposal. But just how formidable or important real events are is a matter of how important a writer cares to make

2

them. Chandler was by nature shy, all his life, and perhaps a bit secretive. Dickens felt his blacking job aged twelve important, and used this material in *David Copperfield*, but Dickens had written *Pickwick* by twenty-four. Dickens laughed and wept at his own readings. But Chandler was cautious, a little suspicious of the friendliness of others, and, in his own words, 'lived on the edge of nothing'.

His childhood was tumultuous enough, with his father leaving his mother for another woman when Chandler was seven, giving him a life-long abhorrence for what he deemed masculine bad conduct. Other emotionally charged events were his being plunged into a matriarchal household in England, composed of mother and a couple of aunts; his enlistment in the Canadian Army during World War I and being sole survivor of a wiped-out platoon; his involvement with Cissy – a married woman when he met her – and the amicable solution on the parts of Cissy, husband, and Chandler, so that Chandler could marry her. Cissy died in her eighties, and Chandler was devoted, at least spiritually, to the last. Their married life, in fact, was very close in the sense that they were always together in one house, though there were no children. Frank MacShane's detailed biography of Chandler mentions that he was often conscious of the difference between his and his wife's ages, anxious about what people might think. Chandler may have strayed from fidelity a few times in his thirties, but he kept a pretty even course for decades afterward, and cracked up only at the last when Cissy died.

All this is the stuff of passion and of novels – one sees it in distilled or distorted form in Dostoyevsky: Fyodor's childhood, his three impor-tant loves – but one sees nothing of life-material in Chandler, except one thin and persistent strain which appears in Marlowe: a sense of decency.

It is almost hard to find, this little strain, like a thread. Because the salient fact about Chandler is that he found his first success in writing tough, popular pulp magazine stories, and his books were outgrowths of this formula fiction. At least he wrote for the best of the pulps at that time, *Black Mask*, and its editors H.L. Mencken and George Jean Nathan, and later captain Joseph Shaw knew what they wanted in a private eye hero.

In the seven books that he wrote with Philip Marlowe as central character, one assumes that Chandler satisfied himself as a writer, and in making a statement on his times. Marlowe's is a realistic view, which makes no comment except perhaps about the weather, or the difficulty of living with or handling a partner, male or female, who has a strong sexual itch. As the blurb-writer said: 'only the action and the conversation'. And the picture of Los Angeles, and of American mores, therefore? The picture is both flat and vivid, like an Edward Burra watercolour or a Leger canvas with heavy, uncompromising black outlines. Chandler could always say a lot in six words.

His first pages are irresistible. If a character has a limp, it is a *limp*, one that nearly knocks the reader over. Chandler said about one book: 'I sort of overdid the similes in that one,' or something to that effect. A few are strained, but the bizarre is Chandler's trademark, as is the abundance of similes, so that when later writers try the same thing, it does not seem original or even natural to them, but mere imitation of Chandler. Chandler's similes gave his writing not only vigour and unforgettable personages, but humour of the wild and insolent American variety.

One looks at Chandler's rather unusual life and wonders how he landed, at fifty-five, in a Hollywood film factory, working on salary, having to turn up daily like everyone else. Chandler had by then, 1943, published *The Big Sleep* and *Farewell, My Lovely* in paperback editions (after the Knopf hardcovers) and his reputation was growing, hence the offer of a job at Paramount as script-writer at $750 per week, 'a sum of amazing magnitude for a man who had been living for a decade on a few thousand dollars a year,' says Frank MacShane. But Chandler was not comfortable and finally worked at home, though still under contract. He had been shy and stand-offish with his colleagues, and appalled from the start by writing from nine to five in an office building, wrestling with what he called impossible and implausible plots. It must have been hell for a mature man who had his own way of doing things. A photograph of this period shows Chandler seated with Billy Wilder on a sofa, Chandler looking weary and maybe bleary but still putting on a tense, polite smile for the cameraman, while Billy leans on one short-sleeved elbow, gazing at Chandler as if asking himself: 'Is this a *Wunderkind* or not?'

And one sees Chandler as not really fitting in, anywhere. He was not wholly American, not English either. With his colleagues he seems to have been ill-at-ease, with potential friends suspicious until he was – somehow – sure of them, and then he is said to have been charming, even warm. Part of the strain must have been due to Cissy at home, who, with her chronic cough and capricious health, couldn't have been a very jolly hostess, one to welcome callers at odd hours of the night in the California style. Chandler is said to have turned guests away at his doorstep if Cissy was not feeling well.

But there remained Marlowe, reasonably sure of himself, of his brains, of his physical strength, even of his morals. Certain jobs Marlowe refused to touch. Marlowe was 'independent', didn't trust cops or their brains or their morals. Blacks were 'dinges', Jews 'sheenies'; and let's hope these colloquialisms don't get bowdlerized from Chandler's works in the name of civil liberties or some such. After all, Marlowe spoke them. Marlowe had a protective crust of cynicism with regard to society, life and love. Marlowe was Raymond Chandler's hero, his Sir Galahad in fact, in twentieth-century form. Chandler himself saw Cissy – maybe not Cissy but a *girl*, and who would she be? – as 'the girl with the corn-flower-blue eyes' as he wrote in a poem before meeting Cissy. So in a sense he surrounded himself with what he needed, Cissy the semi-recluse wife and part mother figure, and Philip Marlowe, a man who could deal with the baser elements of a tough world. It is a kind of religion – idealism, with a hard fist and even a gun to defend it.

The first of these two bastions to disappear was Cissy in 1954. Chandler was then sixty-six. He went again to London, and simply didn't know how to take the acclaim, the welcome he received from his English readers. There was no woman, no female figure at his side, and he was rather lost. The praise, the scotch, the hospitality made him dizzy. He was out of his element, which was that quiet house in La Jolla with his cat, with Cissy ever-present, with their afternoon tea hour and the old daily routine. Chandler's gallant impulses persisted to the last, sometimes wrongly inspired, but never spurned or derided by the two or three Englishwomen who liked and admired him. The end is sad, even tragic: Chandler felt himself alone, aged seventy, at the time when he was most surrounded not merely by anonymous fans but by friends in England and America. He lived four years after Cissy's death, some of the time in hospital because of drink. His bulwarks had gone, and the world had crashed in like a sea. Between Marlowe and Cissy, it would seem that Cissy was the more important.

A book of mine called *Strangers On A Train* gave Chandler fits during his Hollywood script writing period, and from his grave Chandler has given me tit for tat. It is difficult to sum up Raymond Chandler, more difficult than one might think, considering the rather few books he wrote, and their similarity. Chandler seems illogical, his life doesn't fit in with what he wrote. Dickens seems simple and predictable by comparison. Chandler wrote in a letter: 'I suppose all writers are crazy, but if they are any good, I believe they have a terrible honesty.' That sounds indeed like a writer, not funking the job, honest according to his own lights, and willing to work his heart out – maybe in two senses of the phrase.

The Man of Letters
(1908-12)

ERIC HOMBERGER

Raymond Chandler had two literary careers. The first, and least well-known, was an essayist, poet and reviewer in London between 1908 and 1912. We know surprisingly little of Chandler's life in London. There are no surviving contemporary letters or manuscripts, other than galleys and clippings of the printed text of poems. A small anthology of Chandler's early writings was published in 1973. Chandler does not appear in any of the numerous memoirs or biographies of the age, and seems to have passed through London without being very much noticed. As a result it is only possible to approach these years circumstantially, through the career of the man of letters which he adopted, and the traces which this career and his experience in London left in the novels of Chandler's maturity.

After leaving Dulwich College in 1905, Chandler spent a year in France and Germany learning the languages. Upon his return to England he won a clerkship at the Admiralty, which he held for six months. Much to the annoyance of his family, Chandler gave it up and hoped to support himself as a writer. The career of the bookman, the man of letters, was to retain a place in Chandler's imagination. (In a letter to James Sandoe in 1947 he described Desmond MacCarthy as a 'topflight' critic. But then Chandler had a generally low opinion of critics.)

Traces of his first literary career surface in Chandler's sardonic literary allusions in *The Big Sleep*:

> 'I was beginning to think perhaps you worked in bed, like Marcel Proust.'
> 'Who's he?' I put a cigarette in my mouth and stared at her.

There is a running gag in *Farewell, My Lovely* about Ernest Hemingway which Marlowe plays with Sgt Galbraith:

> 'Who is this Hemingway person at all?'
> 'A guy that keeps saying the same thing over and over until you begin to believe it must be good.'

Marlowe, after being drugged by Dr Sonderborg, breaks into half-remembered quotations, allusions, literary jokes:

> I'm in a wild mood tonight. I want to go dance in the foam. I hear the banshees calling. I haven't shot a man in a week. Speak out, Dr Fell. Pluck the antique viol, let the soft music float.

He has *Richard III* on his mind as he speaks to Dr Sonderborg:

> 'Who put me in your private funny house?'
> 'But——'
> 'But me no buts. I'll make a sop of you. I'll drown you in a butt of Malmsey wine. I wish I had a butt of Malmsey wine myself to drown in. Shakespeare. He knew his liquor too. Let's have a little of our medicine.'

Marlowe calls the doctor 'Karloff', and with greater cause is described by Anne Riordan as looking like Hamlet's father. In *The Little Sister*, Marlow answers a hostile Mavis Weld:

> 'Never the time and place and the loved one all together,' I said.
> 'What's that?' She tried to throw me out with the point of her chin, but even she wasn't that good.
> 'Browning. The poet, not the automatic. I feel sure you'd prefer the automatic.'

The irony is rather nasty, reflecting a snobbery which was alien to Marlowe. But it is not Marlowe who knows his way around Shakespeare and Browning, but Chandler himself. The literary allusions reinforce an impression of increasing self-consciousness within the novels. Part of that self-consciousness was caused because Chandler was conducting an argument against the tradition of the detective novel, which he parodied in *The High Window*:

> Taking the evidence piece by piece, putting it all together in a neat pattern, sneaking in an odd bit I had on my hip here and there, analysing the motives and characters and making them out to be quite different from what anybody – or myself for that matter – thought them to be up to this golden moment – and finally making a sort of weary pounce on the least promising suspect.

This was not the reality of Philip Marlowe's Los Angeles. In 1944 he dedicated *Five Murderers* to the editor of *Black Mask*, and to 'the time when we were trying to get murder away from the upper classes, the week-end house party and the vicar's rose garden, and back to the people who are really good at it'. Marlowe, in Chandler's eyes, represented a break with this tradition, as he explains in *The Big Sleep*:

> I'm not Sherlock Holmes or Philo Vance. I don't expect to go over ground the police have covered and pick up a broken pen point and

build a case from it. If you think there is anybody in the detective business making a living doing that sort of thing, you don't know much about cops.

Self-consciousness extends to Marlowe, and the people he meets. When he finds Mrs Fallbrook at the apartment of Chris Lavery in *The Lady in the Lake*, Marlowe tells her that he is Philo Vance, an unemployed lawman doing part-time collection work on car loans. (Vance, the snobbish hero of S.S. Van Dine's thrillers of the 1920s and 1930s, epitomized the unreality of the tradition for Chandler.) Mrs Fallbrook is actually Muriel Chess, returning to the scene of her third murder. She has a gun in her hand, which she says was lying on the stairs. While Marlowe is wondering how to get close enough to take the gun away, she simply hands it to him, and 'sniffed with distaste at the glove which had been wrapped around the butt'. When Marlow appears to doubt her story about finding the gun, she puts her left hand into Marlowe's, 'with a pathetic gesture, like the erring wife in *East Lynne*'. She leaves Lavery's apartment, while Marlowe abstractly admires the perfection of the 'scene' he had just witnessed. (It is one of Chandler's most brilliant.) When Marlow meets Muriel Chess again, having learned that she killed and was now impersonating Crystal Kingsley, she has a gun in her hand. For her benefit, Marlowe translates the 'scene' into its dramatistic elements:

Detective confronts murderer. Murderer produces gun, points same at detective. Murderer tells detective the whole sad story, with the idea of shooting him at the end of it. Thus wasting a lot of valuable time, even if in the end murderer did shoot detective. Only murderer never does. Something always happens to prevent it.

Both detective and murderer are playing roles which are stylized, carefully rehearsed. They have read too many detective stories, seen too many movies. Brody's voice (in *The Big Sleep*) 'was the elaborately casual voice of the tough guy in pictures. Pictures have made them all like that.' Kenny Haste assures Marlowe in *The Little Sister* that

'Your cop friend [Lt Christy French] has been reading pulp magazines.'
'They all do,' I said. 'That's why they talk so tough.'

Later in the book, Lieutenant French warns the tough-talking Moses Maglashan of the Bay City Police not to 'try to steal the picture with that nineteen-thirty dialogue'. Wilde said that life imitates art. Chandler catches the moment when art imitates life imitating art.

Chandler's self-consciousness was often ironic, and sometimes comic. In 'Guns at Cyrano's', a story which he published in *Black Mask* in 1936, an albino gunman is given the show-stopping line 'Shed the heater, rube, or I blow you both in half.' It was the irony of an educated man, tipping the wink to his readers. As Chandler explained (*Raymond Chandler Speaking*), he was attempting to write

> ... on a level which is understandable to the semi-literate public and at the same time give them some intellectual and artistic overtones which that public does not seek or demand or, in effect, recognize, but which somehow subconsciously it accepts and likes. My theory has always been that the public will accept style, provided you do not call it style either in words or by, as it were, standing off and admiring it.

The 'intellectual and artistic overtones' assert Chandler's relations with 'culture'. He was not just a writer of thrillers, but of literature, and was an educated man, indeed a man of letters. Los Angeles, as he understood it, was profoundly alienated from the literary culture of the metroplis. Despite his reservations about the bookman and the tradition of *belles lettres*, we need to see that Chandler was a man divided, neither satisfied with the self-regarding high culture of the man of letters, or content just to write popular thrillers. His cultural ambivalence appears in the novels as self-consciousness and irony.

The man of letters seems so harmless and benign a figure that it is hard to recapture the power which such men once wielded. Before the 1914 war the literary world was not highly specialized. Reviewers were expected to turn their hands to anything which came along. The man of letters was the supreme amateur. Although amateurism is more properly a social than a literary category, we need the idea of amateurism to understand the world of the man of letters, and how far that world is from the present situation, in which there is an elaborate division of critical labour, and in which academic specialization is taken as a matter of course. The Edwardian man of letters did not regard himself as an expert in a 'field', but as a man of taste and sensibility. His relationship to the literary text was comfortable and familiar, exuding a relaxed ease which was significant in a society increasingly uneasy about social change and class conflict. As a critic, the man of letters did not take an interrogatory relationship to what he read. Judging, making discriminations, seemed less important than the need to communicate a genial enthusiasm to his readers. By the end of the war the man of letters was an anachronism. His objective role was that of custodian of a 'high' culture, the possession of which was assumed in the educated and leisured bourgeoisie. He turned his back on crucial developments elsewhere in English society. The extension of literacy, the general rise in the level of education, the emergence of the mass popular press, and popular entertainment, were changing the very meaning of 'culture'. But such developments might just as well have been taking place in the Outer Hebrides as far as the typical man of letters was concerned. They were by taste and inclination likely to pay much more attention to French culture, and preferred their realism in the manner of Zola. The man of letters was there to reassure the bourgeoisie of the authenticity of their claim to culture. In that role he served to confirm prejudices and stem the tide of unwanted innovation. This did not mean that in the work of the man of letters there was an absence of judgment. It was the role itself which seemed increasingly frivolous and indefensible. Eliot, significantly, was the first of the major modern critics who did not make any concessions to the style of the bookman, for whom, in any event, the idea of literature as a 'sacred wood' was laughably inappropriate.

The paradigmatic man of letters was likely to have been educated at Eton and Trinity College, Cambridge (Desmond MacCarthy), Queen's College, Belfast (Robert Lynd), Christ Church, Oxford (S.P.B. Mais); or was to be found among the hordes of self-educated young clerks. Richard Middleton was in the Royal Assurance Exchange Corporation from 1901 to 1907. Edwin Muir worked as a clerk in a law office from the age of fourteen, and held various clerkships until he was thirty-one in 1918. The Georgian poet John Freeman became a junior clerk in the Liverpool Victoria Friendly Society in 1892, where he remained until he became Company Secretary and Director in 1927. Lascelles Abercrombie left Owens College, Manchester, in 1902, and worked as a quanity surveyor. St John Ervine worked as a clerk for an insurance company in London until he was appointed manager of the Abbey Theatre in Dublin. (Wallace Stevens's career with an insurance company in Connecticut suggests the rather more typically English pattern for a literary career at this time.) Chandler's clerkship at the Admiralty was compatible, up to a point, with a literary career, but as his essays suggest, his temperament was romantic enough for him to have grown bored within months of taking up the job. Chandler turned to journalism, and this was probably the most straightforward path to the more congenial work of writing essays and reviews. After coming down from Cambridge, Squire became a parliamentary reporter. Douglas Goldring joined the staff of *Country Life*. The ideal situation was to become a literary editor, like Robert Lynd on the *News Chronicle*, Squire on the *New Statesman*, and Naomi Royde-Smith on the *Westminster Gazette*. The great figures in Edwardian literature were often skilful polemicists and journalists, like Bennett, Wells, Chesterton, Belloc and Shaw. They gave the young writer the impression that journalism and literature were sympathetic partners in the making of a man of letters.

The first problem was to make contact with likely periodicals, and some were openly interested in work by unknown writers. In the *Literary Year Book* for 1915 *The New Age* described itself as 'an independent Socialist review of advanced opinions. Articles mostly such as no respectable paper dare print – until afterwards.' The editor of *The New Age*, A.R. Orage, was willing to print almost anything, but he could not pay his contributors very much money. For someone like Chandler who had given up a clerkship and who had no independent means, there was another obvious place to turn: J.A. Spender's *Westminster Gazette*. Spender had been the contemporary of Curzon and Grey of Fallodon, and had made a name for himself as a Liberal journalist. In 1896 he was invited to become editor of the newly founded *Westminster Gazette*. Spender preached the politics of Rosebery, Campbell-Bannerman, Asquith and Haldane, and after the Liberal victory in 1906 Spender was said to be the most influential political journalist of the day. The young writer might learn from the *Literary Year Book* that the *Westminster Gazette* considered submissions of stories, sketches and general articles, but it was widely known that the best way to approach Spender was through a social contact. A writer might languish in poverty without the right contacts. Chandler saw in Richard Middleton such a figure; Edward Thomas was another.

H.H. Munro, on his return to England after serving in the police in Burma, came to Spender with the recommendation of the cartoonist F.C. Gould. Munro wrote a series of political sketches in the vein of Lewis Carroll for the *Westminster Gazette* which appeared under the pseudonym 'Saki' in 1902. In the same year Munro joined the High Tory

Morning Post as foreign correspondent, but he continued to publish stories in Spender's paper. John Middleton Murry's tutor at Oxford regularly set and judged literary competitions for the *Westminster Gazette*. He was able to introduce Murry to J.A. Spender, who took him on as a reviewer. Murry's first assignment was to review Constance Garnett's translation of *The Idiot* (6 August 1913). By 1914 Murry was writing regularly about new art in London. Chandler's experience was not dissimilar:

> ... J.A. Spender was the first editor who ever showed me any kindness. He was editing *The Westminster Gazette* in the days when I worked for him. I got an introduction to him from a wonderful old boy named Roland Ponsonby Blennerhasset, a barrister with a House of Lords practice, a wealthy Irish landowner ... Spender bought a lot of stuff from me, verses, sketches and unsigned things such as paragraphs lifted from foreign publications. He got me into the National Liberal Club for the run of the reading-room. I was seconded by his political cartoonist [F.C. Gould], a famous man in those days, but I have forgotten his name. I never met him in the flesh.
>
> I got about three guineas a week out of these ...
>
> (letter to Hamish Hamilton, April 1949)

> ... I wrote quite a lot of verses for *The Westminster Gazette* also, most of which now seem to me deplorable, but not all, and a good many sketches, mostly of a satirical nature – the sort of thing Saki did so infinitely better.
>
> (letter to Hamish Hamilton, 11 December 1950)

The literary editor of the *Westminster Gazette* after 1912 was Naomi Royde-Smith, who was sympathetic towards the younger writers. But the whole ambience of the paper was the world of *belles lettres*, and as a result it was less useful to their cause than Ford Madox Hueffer's *English Review* had been between 1908 and 1910. Literary men like Edward Garnett and Edward Marsh could help a younger writer make contact with the paper by introducing them socially. 'I went on Tuesday to Violet Hunt's "at home" at the Reform Club in Adelphi Terrace ... It was very jolly,' wrote D.H. Lawrence on 20 November 1909:

> Elizabeth Martindale & Ellaline Terris and Mary Cholmondeley were there – and Ezra Pound. He is a well-known American poet – a good one. He is 24, like me, but his god is beauty, mine life. He

is jolly nice: took me to supper at Pagani's, and afterwards we went down to his room at Kensington ...

This afternoon I am going up to tea with him & we are going out after to some friends who will not demand evening dress of us. He knows W.B. Yeats & all the Swells.

Contacts could enable a man to earn a living; but the whole point is that they were also a 'way of life', as the career of Rupert Brook suggests. For years one of the most popular features of the *Westminster Gazette* was the literary competitions. While still in the sixth form at Rugby Brooke won a prize for a Sicilian octave in 1905. From 1907 to 1911 Brooke, using a variety of pseudonyms ('Mnemnon', 'Zany', 'Ailouros', 'Arly'), won prizes, or at least had his entries printed, for translations, prose poems, nursery rhymes, parodies, reviews of imaginary books, essays, letters, and exercises in elaborate verse forms. One of the most enthusiastic readers of the *Westminster Gazette* competitions page was a student at the Perse School, F.R. Leavis:

What I remember most vividly is the competitions page. It was assumed there that one not only read, but could plausibly offer to write, French, and I recall that in my regular close perusal of the page I sharpened my sense of the obvious local difference between Baudelaire and Verlaine. (I was very young and not precocious.) I must add, to make the point, that I wasn't tempted to send in any effort to write original Greek verse, though it is significant that it was considered worthwhile to set such tests for competition. The only effort I sent in was a translation of a contemporary war-time poem in German.

Brooke's only major commission from the *Westminster Gazette* came in 1913, when Naomi Royde-Smith learned that he was anxious to travel. (Although Marsh is not named as the source of this information, it sounds rather like the sort of thing he would have done for Brooke.) Brooke's *Poems* were published in 1911, but he had written no other prose than his entries to the *Westminster Gazette* competitions page. But he was Marsh's protégé, and Marsh, in the words of Q.D. Leavis, was 'an innocent blotting-paper to all literary aspirants he met in the right company, particularly good-looking men with fetching manners'. Miss Royde-Smith took a book review by Brooke (of a novel by Compton Mackenzie) to J.A. Spender, and on this basis 'the handsomest young man in England' was off and running. *Letters from America* appeared posthumously in 1916.

15

Brooke's travels in America confirmed his suspicion that American literature was non-existent. Writing to Marsh on 29 June 1913, he remarked that

> It's very queer how utterly they depend upon us for literature. Masefield, Galsworthy, etc., are *precisely* what they are in England. The magazines are filled with English writers, and all the critical articles are about English stuff. They simply don't exist. The Laureateship is discussed ardently and continually.

Brooke's judgment was widely shared by his contemporaries in America, who were queueing up for steerage passage to London. The man of letters was a metropolitan creature, a man of the cultural centre. No matter where he was born or lived in the English-speaking world, his eyes were fixed on London.

While he was an undergraduate at Harvard, Van Wyck Brooks met a man who had been a staff correspondent on *The Times*. Brooks, who 'had delighted in all stories of penniless assaults on literary fame', took with him letters of introduction to various editors when he went to London in 1907. He eventually found work with a journalistic agency and was given a wide variety of assignments, including the abridgement of the autobiography of Geronimo for an English magazine. Despite writing a series of articles on the heroic exploits of journalists, Brooks grew dissatisfied with his work, withdrew to a cottage in Sussex, and wrote *The Wine of the Puritans*. It was published in London in 1908, by which time Brooks had decided to return to America. He had not succeeded as a man of letters, or as a journalist in London. *The Wine of the Puritans* suggests that he had never ceased to think about American culture.

Ezra Pound had just arrived in London when Brooks left. The contrast in their fortunes could not have been more dramatic. Pound had no money, no introductions, no contacts. Within weeks he applied for the vacancy at the Regent Street Polytechnic created by the death of Professor John Churton Collins. He sold a poem to the *Evening Standard* ('Histrion', published on 26 October 1908), and deposited copies of his pamphlet *A Lume Spento* in the bookshops of Elkin Mathews and John Lane. *A Lume Spento* received a glowing review in the *Evening Standard*, but by this time Pound was busy preparing another small pamphlet of poems, *A Quinzaine for this Yule*. It quickly sold out an edition of one hundred copies, and Elkin Mathews reprinted a further one hundred. He also accepted the manuscript of Pound's *Personae*, and began to introduce Pound variously in literary society. He was soon writing to his parents of meeting Laurence Binyon, Maurice Hewlett, Selwyn Image, Ernest Rhys and May Sinclair, who in turn introduced him to W.B. Yeats, Ford Madox Hueffer and Henry James. The reviews of *Personae* confirmed a brilliant early success. It took Pound years to understand that the basis of his success was as much social as literary, but when he did his revulsion was all the more bitter.

Brooks and Pound were Chandler's contemporaries, but being graduates they arrived in London with more highly-coloured expectations of the literary life. Pound dreamed of a bohemian cameraderie. Brooks had been deeply moved by a popular Barrie play about a provincial journalist who comes to the metropolis, makes a great success, and wins the love of a beautiful woman. We know less of Chandler's dreams as a young man.* While a background of Dulwich College and a clerkship in the Admiralty fits the type of the man of letters, his juvenilia doesn't quite have the necessary insouciance. His poems, written as they are in a conventional late-romantic vein, convey a sense of anxiety about the role of the poet and the fate of the Victorian religion of art in an uncaring world. Chandler's essays, mainly written in 1911 and 1912 for *The Academy*, are portraits of various kinds of contemporary literary types: the fop, the genteel artist, the phrasemaker. This sort of thing was already a cliché, even during Chandler's years in London. He demonstrates little originality. The essays seem remarkable only for Chandler's lack of engagement with the literature of the day. Not once in seven essays does he mentioned a book by title, or an author by name. (In a letter to Hamish Hamilton in April 1949, Chandler described these early essays as 'of an intolerable preciousness of style, but already quite nasty in tone'.) His attitude towards the Edwardian and Georgian man of letters is not uncritical: he deplores the amateurish, part-time artist, and wistfully hearkens back to the romantic writer in his garret ('The Genteel Artist'). The over-absorption with verse technique by contemporary poets has resulted in 'futile complication' of craftsmanship for its own sake ('The Literary Fop'). The 'products of a restrained and disciplined art' were in danger of being lost by a public taste which increasingly preferred the exotic ('The Remarkable Hero'). Chandler's essays

* The whole of Chandler's identifiable work of this period has been collected in *Chandler Before Marlowe: Raymond Chandler's Early Prose and Poetry, 1908–1912*, ed. Matthew J. Bruccoli (Columbia: University of South Carolina Press, 1973). Bruccoli is also the compiler of *Raymond Chandler: A Checklist* (Kent State University Press, 1968).

are rather stuffy and humourless. One cannot imagine him successfully conducting a *causerie*, like Jacob Tonson (Arnold Bennett) in *The New Age*, or Solomon Eagle (J.C. Squire) in *The New Statesman*. For all his many failings, Squire could at least see the possibilities in a headline such as 'William Butler Meats And The Garlic Revival', which he came across in the *Connersvile* (Indiana) *Herald*.

The most interesting essays by Chandler are 'Realism and Fairyland' and 'The Tropical Romance'. The latter, in view of Dr Carl Moss's description of Philip Marlowe as 'the shop-soiled Galahad' (*The High Window*), provides a link between Chandler's first and second literary careers. For here Chandler mourns the displacement of the 'artless and incorrigible' adventurer by a psychologically more complex artistry. The more 'degenerate' examples of the type may 'bow and strut in Brummagem-made clockwork detective stories', but the real 'shop-soiled heroes with tarnished morals and unflinching courage' are a disappearing type. Chandler's fears were somewhat excessive. Buchan was on the verge of his major creative phase, and even by 1912 the adventurer was alive and well in the movies.

Chandler might have stuck it out, and gone on to write *Gods of Modern Grub Street* (A. St John Adcock), or *Some Impressions of My Elders* (St John Ervine), or *Figures in Modern Literature* (J.B. Priestley) with that astonishing essay in praise of Robert Lynd. Instead, he went to America, retaining the shadowy dream of a literary culture, the sardonic echo of which was to appear decades later on the lips of Philip Marlowe.

An Aesthete Discovers The Pulps

———

JULIAN SYMONS

Fairyland is Everyman's dream of perfection, and changes, dream-like, with the mood of the dreamer. For one it is a scene of virgin, summery Nature undefiled by even the necessary works of man ... For another it is a champaign, dotted with fine castles, in which live sweet ladies clad in silk, spinning, and singing as they spin, and noble knights who do courteous battle with each other in forest glades; or a region of uncanny magic, haunting music, elves and charmed airs and waters.

That is Raymond Chandler writing in 1912 for *The Academy*.

The man in the powder-blue suit – which wasn't powder-blue under the lights of the Club Bolivar – was tall, with wide-set grey eyes, a thin nose, a jaw of stone. He had a rather sensitive mouth. His hair was crisp and black, ever so faintly touched with grey, as by an almost diffident hand. His clothes fitted him as though they had a soul of their own, not just a doubtful past. His name happened to be Mallory.

That is the opening paragraph of Raymond Chandler's first story for the pulps, 'Blackmailers Don't Shoot', which appeared in *Black Mask*, December 1933.

Between the two pieces lay twenty-one years in time and the Atlantic in distance, but they had a common emotional basis. The Chandler who wrote for the pulps was still a man who dreamed of Fairyland. As I have said elsewhere it is emblematically right that in this first story the detective should be named Mallory, echoing the *Morte d'Arthur*. His carapace of iron (only iron could survive those frequent assaults with cosh and blackjack) conceals a quivering core, and whether his name is Mallory, Carmady, Dalmas or Philip Marlowe, he is truly a knight errant. Chandler's stories about criminals and a detective carried over into an alien field the literary aestheticism of his youth.

Raymond Chandler became a writer for the pulp magazines because he was broke, not because he wanted to write for the pulps. 'Realism and Fairyland' was one of the last pieces he published in England before he gave up the hope of making a literary living there, and he printed nothing in America until 1933. In between he had a variety of jobs, lived with his mother, married a woman eighteen years older than himself as soon as his mother died (his wife Cissy knocked ten years off her age for the marriage register), became vice president of a group of oil companies, drank hard, had affairs, was eventually sacked. At the age of forty-four he had no money and no prospects. At this point he listed himself as a writer in the Los Angeles Directory, and began to study the pulp magazines. It struck him, as he said, that he might get paid while he was learning.

He was not likely, as he must have known, to get paid very much. The pulp magazines, so called because they were printed on wood pulp, began in the nineteenth century with the publication of the Nick Carter stories. The Nick Carter Weekly first appeared in 1891, and like Sexton Blake in England was the product of multiple authors. The chief of them, the bearded Frederic Dey (that is, Frederic Marmaduke Van Rensselaer Day) produced a 25,000 word story every week for years, and did not get rich. In 1929 he shot himself in a cheap New York hotel. Nick Carter's fame endured, and indeed endures, so that when *Detective Story Magazine* began publication in 1915 its editor was named as Nicholas Carter. *Black Mask*, in which most of Chandler's early stories appeared, was founded in 1920 by H.L. Mencken and George Jean Nathan, but did not take on its true character until Captain Joseph Shaw became editor in 1926. During the decade of Shaw's reign the magazine published stories that moved sharply away from the conventional detective story aspect of earlier pulp fiction (Edgar Wallace was one of the stars of *Detective Story Magazine*) to reflect the violence of American society and the vivid colloquialisms of American speech.

Chandler's approach, his background and his age made him a very unusual figure among the pulp writers. Most of them were hacks, although they would have called themselves professionals. They were hard-working, sometimes hard-drinking men who wrote fast and wrote for the money. To make a fair living they had to write a great deal, for the basic rate of one cent a word meant that you had to write a million words to make $10,000 a year. Many of them, like Erle Stanley Gardner, used several names, and some wrote romances and Westerns as well as crime stories. Such a literary netherworld exists in England now, although because there are no magazines its inhabitants write books, turning out ten or a dozen a year to make a reasonable living. In America during the Depression years similar writers worked mostly for the pulp magazines. Few of them had the specialized knowledge of Dashiell Hammett, who had been a Pinkerton agent, but most had familiarized themselves with some aspects of the law and crime, and knew a good deal about firearms. Many of them appeared to write with an ink-dipped cosh rather than a pen.

Chandler resembled them very little. He had read only three or four detective stories when he set out to make a living in the field, and he learned the technique of the crime story in the spirit of a young artist copying masters in the Louvre. He read everything he could find, in particular Hammett, but also Gardner and other pulp writers. He made a detailed synopsis of a Gardner story, rewrote it, compared the result with the original, rewrote it again, and then apparently threw it away. He took what he was doing seriously, because if he had not done so he could not have justified doing it. He was writing for *Black Mask* and *Dime Detective Magazine*, and he knew that what he did was hack work, but he gave to this hack work the care he had devoted to the literary pieces produced for English magazines long ago.

He knew little about the technical aspects of crime, and never bothered to learn, relying instead on textbooks. From the beginning he sensed that for a writer like himself such things were not important, and that any success he won would come through sharpness of language and observation rather than through expert knowledge. In a battling introduction to a collection of his short stories published in 1950, when he had become famous, he defended the pulp crime story by saying that 'even at its most mannered and artificial [it] made most of the fiction of the time taste like a cup of lukewarm consommé at a spinsterish tea-room'. He said also that he wished the stories being republished were better, but that the distinction of the imprint meant that he need not be sickeningly humble, even though 'I have never been able to take myself with that enormous earnestness which is one of the trying characteristics of the craft.' In fact he took himself very seriously indeed, and strongly resented adverse criticism from others, although he was prepared to make it himself. He also made claims for the form in which he was working that must seem over-stated. 'The aim is not essentially different from the aim of Greek tragedy, but we are dealing with a public that is semi-literate and we have to make an art of a language they can understand.' The aim may be similar but the results, as he should have seen, are so different that the comparison is absurd.

Chandler remained by temperament a romantic aesthete. His feebly literary early essays and poems are full of either/ors like science and poetry, romance and realism. Are we to be saved 'by the science or by the poetry of life'? That, he said, 'is the typical question of the age', and he came down on the side of poetry as opposed to science and of romance against realism. Or rather, of realism seen romantically, so that 'any man who has walked down a commonplace city street at twilight, just as the lamps are lit' would see that a true view of it must be idealistic, for it would 'exalt the sordid to a vision of magic, and create pure beauty out of plaster and vile dust'. The phrases echo Chesterton, and also look forward to the famous peroration of 'The Simple Art of Murder' which runs: 'Down these mean streets a man must go ...' It was Chandler's strength, and his weakness, that he brought this basically sentimental aestheticism to the crime stories, so that they had increasingly to be about a romantic hero whose activities gave the novels at least 'a quality of redemption' so that he could think of them as art. That was the weakness. The strength lay in the fact that by treating seriously everything he did Chandler achieved even in his early stories for the pulps more than his fellow practitioners.

To talk about Chandler as a romantic aesthete may make him sound like an intellectual, but in fact he disliked intellectuals and the magazines for which they wrote. In the few meetings I had with him near the end of his life, it was possible to sense his distrust. Was this another of those damned critics trying to get at him? He was fond of using big words like art and redemption, but shied away from such things when they moved from the general to the particular. He could be deeply imperceptive and philistine. 'I read these profound discussions, say in the *Partisan Review*, about art, what is it, literature, what is it, and the good life and liberalism and what is the definitive position of Rilke or Kafka, and the scrap about Ezra Pound getting the Bollingen award, and it all seems so meaningless to me. Who cares?' he wrote to his English publisher Hamish Hamilton. He got on well with fellow pulp writers, partly because they regarded him, as one of them put it, as 'a professorial type, more of an intellectual than most of the other pulp writers I knew'. He was the oldest of them, a year older than Gardner and six years older than Hammett. They respected him, and so made him comparatively at ease. In general he avoided places and people through which he might be involved in literary discussion, preferring to talk to garage men and postal clerks. Other writers, and his opinions of them, he preferred to put on paper.

Second only to romantic aestheticism in giving his work its colour and character was his loneliness. He seems to have been from youth a shy person who found it hard to make friends, and this shyness was accentuated by his marriage to a woman so much older than himself. In these years also they were poor. For a decade Chandler scraped a living, writing for the pulps and publishing crime novels that received critical praise but were far from being bestsellers. They moved from place to place, had few friends, went out little. Out of this loneliness, now and later, Chandler created his best work. When he began to write for films and became involved in the social life of the studios he wrote little, and that little was usually not very good. Shut up in an apartment, with Cissy in the next room and with 'life' making no demands, he sparkled on paper.

The third important element in Chandler's writing was its Anglo-American character. He had been brought up in England, he longed to return (and upon the whole was not disappointed when he came), and the delighted disgust with which he saw California came partly from the contrast between its brash newness and English good taste. When he read Max Beerbohm he felt that he too belonged to an age of grace and taste from which he had been exiled. 'So I wrote for *Black Mask*. What a wry joke.' No doubt he would have felt hopelessly out of place in an age of grace (if such an age ever existed) and would have written ironically about it, but that is not the point. The flavour of his stories is individual partly because, even though, as he said, all the pulp writers used the same idiom, his is filtered through an English lens.

The very intelligent notes on English and American style which he put down in his notebook end with a striking observation of differences in verbal tone:

The tone quality of English speech is usually overlooked. This tone quality is infinitely variable and contributes infinite meaning. The American voice is flat, toneless and tiresome. The English tone quality makes a thinner vocabulary and a more formalized use of language capable of infinite meanings. Its tones are of course read into written speech by association. This, of course, makes good English a class language, and that is its fatal defect. The English writer is a gentleman (or not a gentleman) first and a writer second.

Most of these distinctions seem to me very good ones, but in any case they were important to Chandler. Once he began to write, he became absorbed in the verbal problems involved, in particular the problem of giving an English variability to the 'flat, toneless and tiresome' pattern of American speech. The best of his work is witness to his triumphant success.

Chandler was not a prolific writer. He wrote in all twenty stories for the pulps, at the rate of two, three or four a year. It is true that almost all of them were much longer than the usual story, and that they might almost be called short novels, but even so the output was small. It has been said already that he was poor in the decade after he started to write crime stories. His average yearly earnings during the late 1930s and early 1940s were between one and two thousand dollars. In truth, there was no way of making a reasonable living by writing for the pulps unless you published ten or twelve stories a year. It is a mark of Chandler's integrity as a writer that he refused to do this, or was incapable of doing it, as later he refused to do what he was told in Hollywood when he was employed there at a salary gloriously or ludicrously large compared with his earnings at the time from stories and novels.

About the pulp stories considered as stories there is little to say except that they are not very good. 'Everybody imitates in the beginning,' as Chandler said himself, and the writer he imitated most was Hammett. The young blond gunman in 'Blackmailers Don't Shoot' is obviously derived from Wilmer in *The Maltese Falcon*, the sadistic thug in 'Pick-Up on Noon Street' is based on Jeff in *The Glass Key*, and there are other echoes. Standard scenes and characters appear in most of the stories. There will be at least one night club scene, a variety of villains will appear in every story, and some of them will be gangsters or gamblers who own the night clubs. The hard men who hit the detective over the head will be exceptionally stupid, and the gangsters will be only a little smarter beneath their thin veneer of sophistication. The police will be tough, cynical, and occasionally corrupt. There will be a lot of shooting, with an Elizabethan litter of corpses piled up by the end. At the heart of the trouble there will be a girl, and she is almost never to be trusted, although she may have 'the sort of skin an old rake dreams of' (Rhonda Farr in 'Blackmailers Don't Shoot') or hair that is 'like a bush fire at night' (Beulah in 'Try the Girl') or even hair that 'seemed to gather all the light there was and make a soft halo around her coldly beautiful face' (Belle Marr in 'Spanish Blood'). The women in the short stories are not as deadly as they become in the novels, but they are dangerous enough.

These standard properties are used in a standard way. The detective himself is not much more than a man whose head is harder and whose gun is faster than his rivals'. This is true of Marlowe, who appeared first in 1934, as much as of Mallory or Carmady. But the basic defect

25

of the stories is that the length to which they were written did not fit Chandler's talent. The weakness of his plotting is more apparent in the stories than in the novels. The demand of the pulps, he said later, was for constant action, and if you stopped to think you were lost. 'When in doubt, have a man come through a door with a gun in his hand.' The novels gave more space for the development of situations and the creation of an environment. One of Chandler's great merits was his capacity to fix a scene memorably. He sometimes did this in a phrase, but he could do it even better in a paragraph or a page. The stories did not give him time to create anything of this kind. Everything that did not carry forward the action was excised by editors.

If we read the stories today it is for occasional flashes of observation that got by the blue pencil, and for the use of language. Chandler's ear for the rhythms of speech was good from the beginning, but it developed with astonishing speed. The stories written in the later 1930s, like 'Killer in the Rain', 'The Curtain', 'Try the Girl' and 'Mandarin's Jade' are often as well written as the novels, where the early tales are full of clichés. 'Smart-Aleck Kill' (1934) has eyes that get small and tight, eyes with hot lights in them, eyes that show sharp lights of pain. There are cold smiles playing around the corners of mouths, and mirthless laughter. But within a very few years these have almost all disappeared, and we recognize the sharp cleverness of the novels when we are told that the garage of a modernistic new house is 'as easy to drive into as an olive bottle' or that a smart car in a dingy neighbourhood 'sticks out like spats at an Iowa picnic'.

It was these later and better stories that Chandler cannibalized, to use his own word, to make three of the novels. This was an extraordinary process. Other writers have incorporated early material in a later work, but nobody else has done it in quite this way. Most writers who adapt their earlier work take from it a particular theme or character and jettison the rest. Chandler, however, carved out great chunks of the stories, expanded them, and fitted them into an enlarged plot. Where gaps existed, like spaces in a jigsaw, he made pieces to fit them. It meant, as Philip Durham has said, adapting, fusing and adding characters, blending themes from different stories, combining plots. Much of his first novel, *The Big Sleep*, was taken from two stories, 'Killer in the Rain' and 'The Curtain', plus fragments from two other stories. About a quarter of the book was new material, but the passages from the two principal stories used were much enlarged. There could be no better proof of the limitation Chandler felt in being forced to work within the pulp magazine formula.

Almost all of the enlargements were improvements. They added details of description, vital touches of characterization, or they were simply more elegantly or wittily phrased. They also helped to make the stories more coherent. In 'The Curtain' the detective does not call on General Winslow in his orchid house until chapter three. In the novel Chandler, realizing that this was a splendid starting point, begins with it. (He economically kept chapter one for use years later in *The Long Goodbye*.) The difference in the effectiveness of the two scenes is startling. What was no more than adequate in the story has become memorable in the novel, with the old half-dead General emerging as a genuinely pathetic figure. One would need a variorum text to show exactly how Chandler did it, but here are one or two significant changes. The General is telling Marlowe to take off his coat in the steaming hot orchid house. In 'The Curtain' he says:

'Take your coat off, sir. Dud always did. Orchids require heat, Mr Carmady – like rich old men.'

In *The Big Sleep* this becomes:

'You may take your coat off, sir. It's too hot in here for a man with blood in his veins.'

It is the last sentence that gives real flavour to the bit of dialogue, telling us more about the General than would half a dozen descriptive phrases. And, freed from the blue pencil, Chandler let his love of simile and metaphor run free. The smell of the orchids is not just like boiling alcohol as it was in the story, but like boiling alcohol under a blanket. In the story the General just watches the detective drink, but now 'The old man licked his lips watching me, over and over again, like an undertaker dry-washing his hands.' These are samples from thirty similes or metaphors brought into the scene. Is some of it a little too much? That is obviously partly a matter of taste, but the exuberance of it, the sense of a man using his own talent in his own way for the first time, cannot be anything but enjoyable. This fifty-year-old colt is kicking up his heels in sheer pleasure. And Chandler now is on the lookout for clichés. In 'The Curtain' the General has 'basilisk eyes'. Now they just have a coal-black directness.

The famous, and at the time rather daring, pornographic books passage in *The Big Sleep* appeared first in 'Killer in the Rain'. This too has been transformed. In the story the detective knows in advance of the pornographic book racket, while in the novel suspense is created by our learning with Marlowe the meaning of 'Rare Books'. In the book store he meets a girl with silvered fingernails. A comparison of texts shows the value of Chandler's enlargements.

> She got up and came towards me, swinging lean thighs in a tight dress of some black material that didn't reflect any light. She was an ash blonde, with greenish eyes under heavily mascaraed lashes. There were large jet buttons in the lobes of her ears; her hair waved back smoothly from behind them. Her fingernails were silvered.
>
> She gave me what she thought was a smile of welcome, but what I thought was a grimace of strain.
>
> ('Killer in the Rain')

> She got up slowly and swayed towards me in a tight black dress that didn't reflect any light. She had long thighs and she walked with a certain something I hadn't often seen in bookstores. She was an ash blonde with greenish eyes, beaded lashes, hair waved smoothly back from ears in which large jet buttons glittered. Her fingernails were silvered. In spite of her get-up she looked as if she would have a hall bedroom accent.
>
> She approached me with enough sex appeal to stampede a businessmen's lunch and tilted her head to finger a stray, but not very stray, tendril of softly glowing hair. Her smile was tentative, but it could be persuaded to be nice.
>
> (*The Big Sleep*)

The hall bedroom accent and the businessmen's lunch are the phrases that principally lift this from the commonplace to something hall-marked Chandler, and the elaboration of the scene from one page to three, with a client coming in to change a book, add a lot to its effectiveness.

The blonde reappears, both in story and novel, as the companion of a gangster named Marty (in the book Joe Brody). In both versions the detective gets a gun away from her, she sinks her teeth into the hand with the gun in it, and he cracks her on the head. A couple of grace notes are added in the novel. 'The blonde was strong with the madness of fear', it says in the story. The sentence is rhetorical, and somehow inadequate. In the book it becomes: 'The blonde was strong with the madness of love or fear, or a mixture of both, or maybe she was just strong.' The final touch is not in the story at all. After Brody has handed over some compromising photographs from which he was hoping to make money, the blonde complains of her luck. 'A half-smart guy, that's all I ever draw. Never once a guy that's smart all around the course. Never once.'

'Did I hurt your head much?' Marlowe asks.
'You and every other man I ever met.'

It is a perfect pay-off line, marvellously done.

One could go through the whole book, and through the other novels that have a basis in the stories, showing how, passage by passage, Chandler converted the mechanical effects of the stories into something unique in style and delivery. He discovered his own quality as a writer through the freedom given him by the form of the novel.

The pulp magazines had shaped him, but once he had learned the trade they were a restriction. The novels enabled him to burst the bonds and to express the essential Raymond Chandler: a romantic aesthete and a self-conscious artist, an introvert with the power of catching the form, the tone, the rhythm, of American speech supremely well on paper. In its kind Chandler's mature dialogue is perfect. One cannot see how it could be better done. The stories are not much in themselves, but without them perhaps we should never have had the novels.

Omnes Me Impune Lacessunt

RUSSELL DAVIES

Every page of the Marlowe mysteries bears witness, if only minutely, to the struggle between soul-baring and reticence in Raymond Chandler's mind. If reticence did not win. Philip Marlowe would hardly be the interesting figure he is; but even so, he can occasionally be caught beating his breast with surprising passion:

Uh-huh. I'm a very smart guy. I haven't a feeling or a scruple in the world. All I have the itch for is money. I am so money greedy that for twenty-five bucks a day and expenses, mostly gasolene and whisky, I do my thinking myself, what there is of it; I risk my whole future, the hatred of the cops and of Eddie Mars and his pals, I dodge bullets and eat saps, and say thank you very much, if you have any more trouble, I hope you'll think of me ... I do all this for twenty-five bucks a day ...

If *The Big Sleep* hadn't been Chandler's first try at a full-length novel, I think he might well have toned down this closing speech of his hero's. There is more in it than a reader wants to hear, at least from Marlowe's own lips. But perhaps more distressing than the unnecessary canvassing for pity is the way Marlowe's peroration violates the rule of self-mockery which is a feature of his and Chandler's splendid collusion in the texture of 'their' first-person narrative. Their cooperative coexistence within the prose has proved inimitable, its balance of ironies eluding even the master parodist S.J. Perelman (though *Farewell, My Lovely Appetiser* is scarcely less funny for that). It is really the secret of Chandler's success in his novels, and ultimately the best reason why they continue to be read for profit as well as fun. In so many ways an inhibited character, Chandler seems to have had no trouble at all persuading himself to take risks with his narrative tone. He could let himself into the most dramatic of scenes and cackle invisibly at the action; more remarkably, he would let Marlowe do it for him, as in this double-edged protest from near the climax of *The Lady in the Lake* case, where the detective takes on the role of literary editor:

'I've never liked this scene,' I said. 'Detective confronts murderer. Murderer produces gun, points same at detective. Murderer tells detective the whole sad story, with the idea of shooting him at the end of it. Thus wasting a lot of valuable time, even if in the end murderer did shoot detective. Only murderer never does. Something always happens to prevent it.'

This is a low Hollywood trick, covering up for an implausible scene by having a dig at the whole genre, thereby distracting the audience with the layers-of-reality problem. But somehow Chandler can get away with it. He can use Marlowe to brazen his way through a weak patch in the plot (because of course something *will* happen to prevent Marlowe's getting shot), without endangering Marlowe's separate existence in the imagination. Frank MacShane, in his biography of Chandler, also wondered at this, but his explanation – 'What prevents the reader from mistrusting the voice of the narrator, or doubting its authenticity, is the liveliness of Chandler's language. It is vigorous enough to keep him amused ...' – will not do. Sheer verbal gymnastics would not keep Marlowe going as a credible voice. Most especially, it would not distinguish him as a character, as he surely deserves to be distinguished, from the hundreds of gun-toting nonentities that keep the mass of crime fiction in business.

Yet what makes Marlowe a 'stronger', more interestingly perplexing character than these, paradoxically, is that he is in some ways more like a literal nonentity than any of them. He is not, after all, a hyperactive hero. His influence on events is not often great, despite his talent for being on the spot when they occur. Of *The High Window*, even Chandler himself complained (to Blanche Knopf) that 'the detective does nothing'. Indeed, it is true that Marlowe is more easily defined by what he will not do than by what he will. His scruples define him: the way he won't take more reward than he contracted for, his (somewhat quivering) reluctance to take advantage of lady clients, and so on. But neither the things he does nor those he disdains to do are really responsible for bringing him alive; the things that are done *to him* accomplish this. Perhaps all first-person narrators ought to be roughed up a little in order for us properly to sense the weight of their presence. To Marlowe it happens rather a lot. There is a ritual feeling about the way he is programmatically insulted; the face-slapping he so often gets from frustrated cops (against which there is no appeal) is powerfully debasing. Marlowe is the man it is fun to threaten, and okay to push around. '*Omnes me impune lacessunt*' would be his family motto, if he had one. He more or less said it himself: 'I risk my whole future, the hatred of the cops ... I dodge bullets and eat saps.' (That 'eat' is particularly loaded with masochistic self-abasement.)

By his wounds we know him; but our feeling of Marlowe's being abused cannot remain, either in him or in us, a mere sullen background to events. It builds into a sustaining anger: hence, you might think, the 'hardboiledness' Chandler is famous for, the sour delight he takes in confrontation. But if we look closely at the way Marlowe falls out with the world, traces of a character less phlegmatic and grit-toothed than his begin to emerge. The preoccupations of Chandler's own neurotic personality are revealed, and the sharp tang of paranoia – currently flavour-of-the-decade in American popular art – is in the air. Why, for example, are there virtually no 'gatherings' of people in Chandler's novels? He could not manage populous tableaux at all, and it is as much as he can do to keep three people alive on the page at the same time. 'A crowded canvas just bewilders me,' he wrote. 'Give me two people snotting each other across a desk and I'm happy.' What evidence there is suggests that behind this odd temperamental limitation (perfectly consistent with Chandler's behaviour in life: he was at his worst on large-scale occasions) lay an exhausting obsession with the mechanics of acquaintanceship – first impressions, liking and hating instinctively. Chandler seems to have found it hard to get beyond the miniature rivalries and truces implicit in personal contact (what the modern jargon-word calls 'chemistry'), and sometimes the subject took an obsessional hold on him. *The High Window* provides an almost comical concentration of examples. Within five pages, at the beginning of the book, Marlowe's unattractive client, Mrs Murdock, has challenged him: 'You don't like me very well, do you?' ('Does anybody?' is his reply); her secretary has pointedly suggested to him: 'Perhaps I don't like virile men'; and the son of the house has snarled at Marlowe: 'I'll try hard, but I don't think I am going to like you.' 'I'm screaming,' retorts our boy, 'with rage and pain.' But before the book is out, he almost will be.

After a surge of plot, people once again begin to tell Marlowe they are not going to like him 'one damned little bit'; they even start assuring him that other characters, not present, don't like him either. And when Mrs Murdock further adds that she doesn't like Marlowe's 'tone', the poor man breaks out in a sweat of comprehensive disgust: '"I don't blame you," I said. "I don't like it myself. I don't like anything. I don't like this house or you or the air of repression in the joint"', and so on. One might suppose this takes the subject about as far as it can go – almost into burlesque – but within a few pages it is being sighingly aired again by Mrs Murdock's son: 'I suppose I like to be liked.' But he realizes that in Marlowe's case he has drawn a blank. 'Well – I guess

I can take it that you don't like me.' Unsweetened by this, Marlowe rounds off the book with another broadside against the Murdocks: 'I don't like her, I don't like you. I don't like this house. I didn't particularly like your wife. But I like Merle. She's kind of silly and morbid, but she's kind of sweet too. And I know what has been done to her in this damn family for the past eight years.' Out of a fantastic mêlée of anti-pathies comes fellow-feeling at last for the one substantial character in the book who, like Marlowe himself, has been unjustly punished.

By giving almost all the characters a share of it, Chandler has made misanthropy a semi-conscious theme of *The High Window*, which prob-ably accounts for its relative failure at the deeper levels of interest. In circumstances where *everybody* seems imprisoned in his own mysterious resentments, and nobody has the confidence of his own corruption, Marlowe is bound to appear a less exceptional being. But in the better books, he shows up in the strange isolation of his uncivic nature. He harbours, it seems to me, a malice born of personal disillusion that has almost nothing to do with the crime-world he moves in. Of course, Mar-lowe and Chandler do reserve a special contempt for rich hypocrites, sold-out lawmen and bribable politicians, and in a practical way the books are all about these more or less political venalities. (And thus they have gained in appeal of late. Nothing is more fashionable now than the scepticism Chandler voiced in 1945: 'P. Marlowe doesn't give a damn who is President; neither do I, because I know he will be a politician.') But beneath the social cynicism of the plot-surface, there is always the story of a man, Marlowe, who goes through life hating his fellows out of disappointment, because they are not what he wants them to be – the ideal woman, or the mirror-image man of conscience. The fact that Terry Lennox, with his very Chandlerian weaknesses, so nearly fits the bill in *The Long Goodbye* makes that book the most bitter-sentimental of all.

The reasons why Chandler nourished such high and necessarily doomed expectations of his fellow men are lost now in his personal his-tory, and beyond reconstruction. But his writings strongly suggest that he had a hard time controlling his exaggerated response to physical appearance. The number of beautiful, worthless women and fine-look-ing evil men in his stories testifies to his lasting puzzlement over this matter, in particular as to whether beauty is truth or perfidy. Try as he may to resist, he cannot avoid being seduced into ambiguous atmo-spheres whenever the problem arises. Whole reinterpretations of

Chandler's psychology have been built on moments like the one in *The Lady in the Lake*, where, after a typically snarling, intimate interview, Marlowe leaves the man Lavery ('he had a terrific torso and magnificent thighs') with the words: 'So long, beautiful hunk.' It is hard to see how one would rid this of its worrying traces of admiration, even if one were to read it with all the sarcasm Dick Powell, James Garner and Robert Mitchum could muster between them. But if Marlowe's response is ambiguous here, there is at least some saving conflict going on between his aesthetic and his moral senses. On the rare occasions when he meets somebody he likes, there is nothing to get in the way of the rising sap, the hot flush. When Red, the boatman, appears in *Farewell, My Lovely*, the prose becomes suffused with approval, and begins to radiate a disconcertingly physical warmth: 'I looked at him again. He had the eyes you never see, that you only read about. Violet eyes. Almost purple. Eyes like a girl, a lovely girl. His skin was as soft as silk. Lightly reddened, but it would never tan. It was too delicate.' No wonder alliances struck up in terms like these have raised suspicions of a homosexual yearning on Chandler's part. One can feel him at such moments falling in love with his own fantasy; he emerges almost as a decadent figure.

His readers sensed as much, though they pinned the fault, not unnaturally, on Marlowe. Chandler defended him robustly. 'If seeing dirt where there is dirt constitutes an inadequate social adjustment, then Philip Marlowe has inadequate social adjustment,' he wrote – knowing that on this point he could be safely defiant. If beauty tended to send Marlowe/Chandler haywire, with ugliness they were sure of themselves. The social blemishes Marlowe spends his life confronting undeniably exist, are undeniably ugly. What honourable man could be other than out of temper with such a horrible milieu? Yet behind even this unexceptionable argument there are neurotic sensibilities hiding away. By 'dirt' Chandler habitually meant corruption, but it doesn't take a fanatical Freudian to sense in his works the marked attraction/repulsion that literal filth holds for him. Despite Marlowe's own shabby style of living, he is unfailingly shocked – one might even say thrilled – by squalor; he can run his hand up and down a door frame (in Jessie Florian's house) and shiver: 'Just touching it made me want to take a bath.' The description of the lobby of the Fulwider Building in *The Big Sleep* is, in a way, a poem to muck ('A case of false teeth hung on the mustard coloured wall'); and there is no end to the conclusions a sexologist might draw from the fact that within seven lines, Chandler draws attention to 'a traffic cop in shining black rubber from boots to cap'; 'my rubber heels', slithering on the pavement; and the 'well-missed spittoon on the gnawed rubber mat'. It is not to be ignored that at the end of the next paragraph, where the mood is still unbroken, the narrator observes that 'In a shadowy angle against the scribbled wall a pouched ring of pale rubber had fallen and had not been disturbed. A very nice building.'

The worst of this extreme aesthetic touchiness – which, it becomes increasingly plain, is the one area in which Chandler is unable to suppress his own feelings in favour of Marlowe's likely ones – is that it extends to people as well. They can be just as slimy as doorposts, in Chandler's eyes, and he can make Marlowe just as scathing about them. Worse than scathing. It is downright unpleasant to hear Marlowe sneer, in *The High Window* again (why did Chandler think *The Little Sister* his worst-tempered book?), at 'the fat greasy sensual Jew with the tall stately bored showgirl', where the beauty-and-the-beast inappropriateness implied is even more offensive than the choice of adjectives. The kindest thing one can say about Chandler's racially tinged observations is that he does not pursue them far below the level of physical distaste. Blacks are accorded the same arm's-length treatment; Chandler's preferred terms for them are 'shine' and 'dinge', which speak for themselves. Sheer unthinking (hygiene-based) snobbery is all that is involved here, perhaps; Chandler appears to have been genuinely surprised by the protests he aroused, and responded, with typically doomed gentlemanliness, by including both a sympathetic/pitiable Jew, Mr Edelweiss, and a comical/cultured black, Amos the chauffeur – patronized figures both – in his last full-length novel, *The Long Goodbye*.

Too self-absorbed to calculate such effects with success, Chandler was well aware of his own imperfections as a human being, but the ones he advertised were usually those which, with the aid of a typewriter, could be translated into virtues. 'At times I am extremely caustic and pugnacious, at other times very sentimental. I am not a good mixer because I am very easily bored, and the average never seems good enough, in people or anything else.' These are very much the qualities Marlowe displays, but we tend not to hold them against him, because he strikes us as a man with higher personal standards than life permits him to live by. But what we have lacked – until very recently – has been an example of Chandler's operating these standards without a Marlowe, or Marlowe-substitute, to filter them through: a piece of writing which would indicate at what precise distance from the reality of Chandler's moral being Marlowe stands. A prize example of unencumbered Chandler, however, has now escaped from the files; and to those who have long suspected that Marlowe's stolid rectitude is a cover-up job, it will come as more of a relief than a surprise.

The short story 'English Summer', as recently unveiled, turns out to be one of the most revealing pieces Chandler wrote. He returned to it near the end of his life in hopes of turning it into a play, but we know from his famous typewritten 'statement of aims', committed to paper in March 1939, that it was a well-developed notion even then. Chandler saw it as no small part of his future: 'a smash hit', he predicted, '... properly written, written up to the hilt but not overwritten'. His preliminary outline does not promise well, though:

> *English Summer.* A short, swift, tense, gorgeously written story verging on melodrama, based on my short story. The surface theme is the American in England, the dramatic theme is the decay of the refined character and its contact with the ingenuous, honest, utterly fearless and generous kind of American of the best type.

Which sounds a lot like a gumshoe Henry James in the land of Ronald Firbank. But no such luck. 'English Summer' is worse than that. Under the subtitle 'A Gothic Romance', it runs to twenty pages, two weirdly contrasting sexual fantasies, and a dreadful variety of tones. But it leaves you in no doubt of its urgent personal importance to the author.

The narrator, John Paringdon (Chandler's letters apparently say Faringdon, which does seem more likely), is an American of no fixed mood, staying at an English country cottage. His hosts are the Crandalls: Edward, a big, handsome, bibulous hunting-and-golfing type; and his wife Millicent, whose several ways of being 'very lovely' are itemized, ending with the lovely arms – 'and they seemed to know it, without, as it were, her knowing it'. The atmosphere by now is pretty sodden with Paringdon's unspoken devotion to this strangely coordinated and ceramic personage.

Having failed to interest her in a rowing expedition on the lake, Paringdon takes her motherly advice ('Run along now, and don't be too late for tea') and goes by himself. It is while he is tying up the boat that she – another she – appears behind him on a big black horse. 'She wore a black riding habit, a white hunting stock at her throat, and the horse looked wicked as she sat astride of him. A stallion.' And a wonderfully arousing spectacle, matched in Chandler's novels (if you forget the horse, whose name is Romeo) only by the deranged homosexual youth Earl, who appears similarly garbed, interestingly enough, in *The Long Goodbye*; and the lady from *The Little Sister* with the coal-black jodhpurs, the 'amigo'-studded conversation and scarcely containable nymphomania: Dolores Gonzales, probably the most preposterous figure, and certainly the most adolescent-prurient female, in all the Marlowe stories. When last heard of, Miss Gonzales was described as 'Reeking with sex. Utterly beyond the moral laws of this or any other world I could imagine'; and much the same self-condemning definition, with due allowance made for her Englishness, must apply to Lady Lakenham – for it is she, or will turn out to be, once she has got the biddable Paringdon home to her rotting, plundered Elizabethan mansion, Lakeview. The sexual prospects, however, which had seemed likely to entail a masochistic role for Paringdon, to judge by the riding-crop Lady L. is forever twirling, dissolve into a comfortable orthodoxy in the chapter-closing moments. Her costume having done its hormone-mobilizing work, the lady gasps 'Please, oh please' in the ultimate clinch, revealing at last the protectable supplicant inside the man-eating guise.

'English Summer' by this stage is an obviously unrescuable item, and it would be neither fair nor profitable to dwell on it if the way Chandler achieved its resolution did not reflect so interestingly that inner conflict which gave Marlowe his being. Paringdon now returns to the Crandalls', where Edward has seemingly passed out in an upstairs bedroom, and Millicent is in an unspecifiable mood, odd enough to cause her to 'ripple from head to foot'. Checking on Edward's condition upstairs, Paringdon discovers him to be dead, obviously killed by the rippling lady. What follows upon this discovery is a most extraordinary conversation, the emotional centrepiece of 'English Summer'. Chandler articulated the thought behind it in a letter to Helga Greene: 'He (Paringdon) has, according to his code and mine, incurred an obligation, and we Americans are a sentimental and Romantic sort of people, often wrong of course, but when we have that feeling we are willing to destroy ourselves rather than let someone down.' This sounds reasonable enough; but in the event, moral considerations of the codified kind are swept aside by the feelings that burst uncontrollably out of the passage. Deprived of the influence of Marlowe's moderating irony-cum-bravado, it seems terribly unguarded, psychologically, with a combination of clumsiness and daring that Chandler simply could not have perpetrated in his crime-novels. Its clash of tones is bizarre:

'No,' I said, without breath. 'Never. This is easy. Will you play it my way?'

She stood up all in one smooth motion and came to me. I took her in my arms. I kissed her. I touched her hair.

'My knight,' she whispered. 'My plumed knight. My glistening one.'

'How?' I asked, pointing into the drawer at the gun. 'They'll test his hand for powder nitrates. That is, leakage of gas when the gun is fired. It's something that stays in the skin for a while and makes a chemical reaction. That has to be arranged.'

She stroked my hair. 'They will, my love. They will find what you mean. I put the gun in his own hand, and held it there, and soothed him. My finger was over his finger. He was so drunk he didn't even know what he was doing.'

She went on stroking my hair.

'My plumed, glistening knight,' she said.

I wasn't holding her now; she was holding me. I squeezed my brains slowly, slowly. Into a clot.

'It may not make a very good test,' I said. 'And they might test your hand as well. So we must do two things. Are you listening to me?'

'My plumed knight!' Her eyes shone.

This is a uniquely strained piece of writing, and who can wonder at it, given all the guilts and temptations the scene throws up. As Millicent begins her soft exhalations of worship, the feeling is irresistible that Chandler's mind finds them thrilling; to have the ego thus exquisitely massaged is obviously a powerful fantasy for him. But what does he do, having offered his hero this ultimate gratification? He cannot go through with it. It's as though a moral thermostat cut in to cancel the mood, and Paringdon becomes the hard, practical man who thinks, however utterly-fearless-and-generously, in terms of hard consequences. He becomes, in fact, Marlowe – essentially passive, but serviceable, an organizer of reality on behalf of those to whom he feels loyalty, even when they have done wrong (cf Moose Malloy). Paringdon chooses, too, a Marlowe-like solitude. Escaping with a proper Gothic shudder ('I pried myself loose from her and left that house'), he flees to the edge of Dartmoor. It's amusing – in a better-made tale it would be more than that – to note that the Scotland Yard man who comes to entice him back to a forgiving civilization is called Inspector Knight.

'English Summer' is slung between two great complementary impulses in Chandler: a self-effacement turning to self-pity, and a desire, almost a demand, to be admired. In this, it is wholly characteristic of the 'unguarded' Chandler writings. Whenever he is unchaperoned by Marlowe, these twin instincts shoot to the surface; the first, for example, in a poem of Chandler's which closely parallels what real-life feeling there is in 'English Summer':

> I do not think I shall touch her hair
> Nor lay groping fingers on her unforgotten eyes,
> Perhaps I shall not even speak to her,
> But presently turn away, choked with an awful longing,
> And go off under the grave English trees,
> Through the gentle dusk,
> Into a land called Death.

(Or Cornwall, as the case may be.) And the second in 'A Couple of Writers', another of Chandler's sad 'uncommercial' fragments, featuring the drunken author Hank: '"I wish I had a dog," he said to the night. "Why do I keep wishing that? I guess I need someone to admire me."'

But the fact of being humanly admired, as Paringdon's story shows, cannot finally be faced. It is too 'gorgeous', and has to be pre-paid in guilt (Millicent's murder). Paringdon flees the guilty embarrassment of it, looking more and more like Marlowe as he goes; and I don't think it's unreasonable to say that Marlowe represents Paringdon's flight turned into a routine, a style of life. Marlowe has already banished himself to a spiritual Cornwall before we meet him. He is a man in whom the liveliest hopes have died; but he maintains himself in the face of a world which has let him down. For this he claims our admiration. But it is self-pity that allies him intimately to Chandler. You can see it in the studied dullness of his ordered life: the bottle in the desk, the (admittedly good) coffee in the morning, the trivial round of 'missing-persons' business. It's a complete metaphor for the writer's life – but a writer in retreat from the sensuality of the world outside. Marlowe inherits Chandler's fear. His role in life, so often seen as a matter of chivalric gestures, is a more desperate business. He is maintaining a self-preserving critique on behalf of bedazzled mediocrity against social evils

41

which, be they blatantly ugly or perversely beautiful, always carry with them a fatal glamour that rouses his creator's senses. In effect, Chandler has postulated a burnt-out man who can resist the worst of his fantasies – hence the page-by-page struggle, friendly but real, between them. Behind every pale pink indiscretion of the censorious Marlowe, there may be a swelling purple dream of Chandler's. Or is 'English Summer' a unique and unindicative self-indulgence?

I think not. On his way to Cornwall, John Paringdon stops for a few nights at an anomymous lodging-house in Bloomsbury, an area 'haunted' by 'white-faced specters' – prostitutes. Four other guests, besides Paringdon, are mentioned. 'There was a man at the digs who played Bach, a little too much and a little too loud; but he did it for his own soul.' There were also 'two young wooden butterflies who thought of themselves as actors'. And 'there was a lonely old man with a poised, delicate face and a filthy mind'. I wonder who *he* was?

On The Fourth Floor of
Paramount

INTERVIEW WITH BILLY WILDER

BY IVAN MOFFAT

Wilder: It's a very peculiar thing, you know, in all the forty years plus that I have been in Hollywood, when people have come up and asked questions – newspaper men, researchers, or letters from all over the place – the two people that I've been connected with whom everyone is most interested in are Marilyn Monroe and Raymond Chandler. There is some kind of fascination, as well there might be, because they were both enigmas. I knew them well – I made two pictures with Monroe and I wrote and lived on the fourth floor of Paramount for a long time with Chandler – and they were, indeed, enigmas.

I had been a writer at Paramount, teamed with Charles Brackett on many pictures. I had been writing for Mitchell Leisen and Lubitsch – all kinds of things – and one day Joe Sistrom, who was on the production staff there, and was indeed to be the producer of the picture I made with Chandler (though he did not take any credit because he was very insulted that they only wanted to give him the associate-producer credit and he said 'get lost') well, he brought me a story from the old *Liberty* magazine, which is long since deceased. James M. Cain, who had written a most successful novel called *The Postman Always Rings Twice* and who was very much *en vogue*, wrote a short story in two or three or four instalments for *Liberty* magazine called 'Double Indemnity'; and it was in texture, and even in content, an echo of the much better *The Postman Always Rings Twice* (which was owned by MGM and done after *Double Indemnity* with Garfield and Miss Turner; it was a very poor picture, if I say so myself, as shouldn't – the better novel made the poorer picture).

Now Mr Sistrom came and said 'Read that' ['Double Indemnity'], and I read it, and I got very, very excited about it and Charles Brackett, with whom I had been working, was off on some other thing, so it just worked out that I was free – by this time I was already a director, having directed *The Major and the Minor* and *Five Graves to Cairo* – and Sistrom said, 'Well, who do you want to work with on the script?' And I said, 'Let's take Cain.' But Cain – and this is very Hollywood – was working at Fox on a picture called *Western Union*, so Sistrom said, 'Look, there is another writer around town, who writes kind of good – good dialogue and sharp

44

characters – he is a sort of mystery writer who graduated from the *Black Mask* magazine, as has Dashiel Hammett and a lot of other very good writers, and he has sort of the smell of Southern California, where *Double Indemnity* plays – Los Feliz Boulevard and the Pasadena Station and insurance companies downtown and so on.'

Well, we called for Mr Chandler, who appeared in the office of Mr Sistrom. He had never been inside a studio; he had never worked on a picture; he had no idea what the hell the whole thing was about. Sistrom asked him to read the story, which he did, and he came back and said yes, he would like to do it, could he see what a screenplay looked like? So we gave him a screenplay. He had that idiotic idea, you know, that if you know about 'fade in' and 'dissolve' and 'close-up' and 'the camera moves into the keyhole' and so on, that you have mastered the art of writing pictures. He had no idea how these things were done. I remember well what he said: 'I would be interested ˙if you think I am the right man; but this is already Tuesday; I cannot promise you the script until next Monday.' And we looked at him as though he was a maniac. He didn't know that he was going to work with me. Then he said: 'I want a thousand dollars.' We just looked at each other.

He left and he did indeed come back on Monday, having done about eighty pages of script. It was eighty pages of technical drivel – you know, fade-ins and dissolves and all very fancy and full of things he had seen in movies and had found out through the script we had shown him. And we said, 'All right, relax Mr Chandler, this is the way it's going to happen. You will be working with Mr Wilder, who is a writer too; you will be writing together.' He was sort of taken aback. It wasn't the thing for a man who was a novelist to have a collaborator. Then he repeated that he wanted a thousand dollars. We said, 'None of that thousand dollar shit. You are going to get 750.' And he said, '750, I will not work for 750.' We said, 'No, relax, 750 a *week*. Just relax, you are going to get 750 a week.' And he said, 'Oh, really? Then it only goes two or three weeks?' And we said, 'No, fourteen weeks. You don't know how scripts are written.'

And that is the way it started and he sat down and we started working. But as we all know, and he would be the first person to tell you, he was a very peculiar, a sort of rather acid man, like so many former alcoholics are. He was on the wagon, and he was also married to a woman who was considerably older than he was. Suddenly discipline sort of came into his life, because he had to come in the morning and we would write every day, and I would be pacing up and down, and we would have yellow pads. But he didn't really much like me, ever.

Moffat: Why not?

Wilder: Well, to begin with there was my German accent. Secondly I knew the craft better than he did. I also drank after four o'clock in the afternoon and I also, being young then, was fucking young girls. All those things just threw him for a loop. But I thought that he had an enormous talent and we got along fine. Except one day, after about the first three weeks, I remember, Mr Chandler did not show up, and I was waiting and waiting – he should have showed up at nine – and finally at around eleven-thirty or twelve, I went up to Sistrom and I said, 'Shall we find out what happened to Chandler? He didn't show up.' And he said, 'I will tell you what happened to Chandler, he has sent me a letter.' It was a letter of complaint against me: he couldn't work with me any more because I was rude; I was drinking; I was fucking; I was on the phone with four broads, with one I was on the phone – he clocked me – for twelve and a half minutes; I had asked him to pull down the Venetian blinds – the sun was beating into the office – without saying 'please'. A whole list of complaints. Se we got him to come in, and said, 'Come on, cut our that shit, come on for Christ's sake, we don't have court manners here.' And I apologized: I will never talk, I will never drink in your presence, and so on. And we finished the script. But in a book of little paragraphs that were put together about Chandler later, he said that he had a miserable time with me because I was a son-of-a-bitch. However, he said that all he ever knew about pictures was what he had learned from me. So there was a kind of resentment. Subsequently he stayed on.

Moffat: Stayed on in what way?

Wilder: He stayed on at Paramount and wrote about three or four more pictures, but not with me anymore.

Moffat: Had you read any of his work?

Wilder: I did read some before I met him. I read *The Brasher Doubloon* which was re-titled, and I read two or three of his novels. They were no great structural things. They had nothing to do with the Conan Doyle or Agatha Christie type of superb plotting. They weren't even as well plotted as Dashiel Hammett; but, by God, a kind of lightning struck on every page. How often do you read a description of a character who says that he had hair growing out of his ear long enough to catch a moth? Not many people write like that; and the dialogue was good, and the dialogue was sharp.

Moffat: How soon after you worked together did he start to learn about scripts?

Wilder: Well, there was not much to learn, because I would just guide the structure and I would also do a lot of the dialogue, and he would then comprehend and start constructing too. I told him very quickly, 'Look, I'm going to direct the picture so none of that fade-in and none of those camera tricks: just let's write characters and situations and words.' And he learned that. And he was just an extraordinary man, you know.

Moffat: What did Chandler think of *Double Indemnity*?

Wilder: In the first preview that we had in Westwood Village, James Cain was standing in the lobby and he put his arms around me and said that it was the first time that somebody had done a good job on any of his stuff, and he kissed me. Chandler sneaked out because he did not want to be seen with his wife.

Moffat: Why?

Wilder: Because she was a grey-haired lady.

Moffat: He was ashamed of her, was he?

Wilder: People would kind of turn to him and say 'Oh, is this your mother?' You know, that kind of situation.

Moffat: Was she sort of a mother figure?

Wilder: No, she was a mother image, she *looked* like a mother. When I did see him he would kind of growl. He was a very difficult man.

Moffat: Bad tempered?

47

Wilder: Yes, bad tempered – kind of acid, sour, grouchy – I don't know. There was just something about him, you know. But I much preferred *that* to somebody who is light of foot, grace-ful, full of jokes, but totally incompetent, you know. Give me a collaborator like Chandler any day.

Moffat: Did he like the story to start off with?

Wilder: Yes, he liked the story. That's why he agreed to do it. Of course he was not too complimentary about Cain, and we improved it quite a bit. Cain didn't have that kind of sting in his dia-logue. Also I must say that Chandler's great strength was a descriptive one. There are very few people who can get the flavour of California. It's very peculiar, you know, that the only person who caught the Californian atmosphere in prose was an Englishman – Chandler. And the only person who caught it on canvas was also an Englishman by the name of Hockney. No one else can paint California; he can.

Moffat: But why, after all, the film was a tremendous success and a tremendous classic, why didn't you and he work again together?

Wilder: I was kind of on a loan-out, you know. I was cheating on Charles Brackett. I came back and we did *Lost Weekend* right after this. As for *Double Indemnity* it was extraordinarily diffi-cult to cast because, in those days, for a big star to play a murderer or a murderess – though Barbara Stanwick in-stantly knew that it was a great part, and she volunteered – was nearly impossible. I went crazy looking for a man to play the part. I went to every single star at Paramount and nobody would touch it. I remember I went one day, in my despair, and told the story of the film to George Raft. And he was sitting there looking bewildered and he kind of interrupted me once in a while and then he said, 'When do we have the lapel?' And I said, 'What?' And he said, 'Well, go on.' And I went on, and then he asked again, 'Where's the lapel?' And he would not explain to me what this meant until I came to the end, and he said, 'Oh, no lapel.' I said, 'What is the lapel?' He said, 'You know, at a certain moment you turn the hero's lapel and it turns out that he's an FBI man or a policeman or someone who works for the government – a good guy really.'

Moffat: They call that a lapel?

Wilder: Yes.

Moffat: I've never heard that, have you?

Wilder: Never.

Moffat: The trouble with George Raft is that he didn't have a lapel. He got kicked out of England for not having one.

Wilder: Ultimately I got Mr Fred McMurray to play the part. It wasn't easy. He said, 'Look, Christ, I'm doing comedy. I'm a saxophone player, I do little comedies with Carole Lombard.' I said, 'You've got to take this big step,' and I finally talked him into it. Later he said that it was the favourite part he'd ever played. He's a very nice guy, and I like him very much, and a very good actor. There are also two of the best scenes that I've ever shot in my whole life still in the vaults at Paramount – one was the execution of Fred McMurray in *Double Indemnity*.

Moffat: You mean to say they executed him in the movie?

Wilder: Yes, I shot a whole scene in the gas chamber, which we never needed. Everything was reconstructed very authentically. We completely rebuilt the gas chamber and we had the bucket and the pellets dropping in the gas, and outside that glass door, you know, where the doctor has got the stethoscope through that thing listening to see whether he is alive or not. And there are some spectators, and he looks and sees Edward G. Robinson watching, and there's a look between the two, and then Robinson leaves and strikes a match on the nail of his thumb. But then the scene was unnecessary. We ended it when he collapses and you hear, in the distance, the sound of the ambulance or of the police car. That was the end of the picture.

Moffat: There was that lovely scene in the film when Edward G. Robinson is detailing all the different kinds of suicide. Who did that one?

Wilder: We wrote it together. But that was not the difficult bit. The difficult bit was to memorize it. Robinson did that in one day, one and a half pages of it.

Moffat: To get back to Chandler – you may not have worked amicably but you worked equally?

Wilder: Yes, we worked well. We would discuss a situation. Once we had the broad outline, we added to and changed the original story and arrived at certain points of orientation that we needed. Then we would start scene by scene, and we started with dialogue, and then with transition. And he was very good at that, just very, very good.

Moffat: Did you ever laugh together?

Wilder: Very rarely. He would just kind of stare at me. I was all that he hated about Hollywood. He'd never seen an animal like this before.

Moffat: Also you were much younger.

Wilder: I was much younger. And he was kind of bewildered, you know; and I was much more at ease with the medium because this was the first piece of pottery he had ever done, and by this time I had done thousands of pieces of pottery – pots to piss in, pots with Mexican designs, every kind of pot went through my hands. But for him, it was a new medium.

Moffat: What effect do you suppose working with you on *Double Indemnity* had on his life, and on his career? He hadn't been involved in movies before then.

Wilder: I guess he could never find his way back to novel writing. He could not sit down any more unless he sort of smelled some kind of activity and studio companionship. You remember how it was on the fourth floor of Paramount – writers sitting around drinking coffee or pinching secretaries' asses, or whatever it was. He found it very difficult, I guess, to go back to a lonely life with just a wife and a typewriter and to switch back again to a completely different medium. And he was making exceedingly good money, not the sort of money that you have to wait for while you are writing a novel – this was instant weekly money.

It's a very peculiar thing, the business about serious writers who have followed the lure of Hollywood. Very few of them took it seriously; to them it was easy money, and they always pooh-poohed it. And they were always slightly ashamed. I'm talking now about Scott Fitzgerald, whom I knew – he was also on the fourth floor at Paramount. And Faulkner, he spent some time there.

Moffat: When did you last see Chandler?

Wilder: Must have been shortly after *Double Indemnity*, because I did *Lost Weekend* and lost sight of him. Then there was the war and, when I came back, he was around, I saw him, but we were not too chummy, ever.

Lost Fortnight

JOHN HOUSEMAN

Just don't get too complicated,
Eddie. When a guy gets complicated
he's unhappy. And when he's unhappy —
his luck runs out. ...

Raymond Chandler, *The Blue Dahlia*

Raymond Chandler was fifty-seven when he risked his life for me. By then most of his books had been written. His creative days were almost over, but his great success was just beginning; royalties were coming in now, followed by movie sales. For the first time in many years Chandler and his wife were able to enjoy such modest Southern Californian comforts as they desired.

Ray appeared at the Paramount studio in Hollywood soon after I got there; he came at the invitation of Joe Sistrom to work with Billy Wilder on dialogue and to supply the Los Angeles atmosphere for a movie called *Double Indemnity*, which made a lot of money and received an Academy nomination. By then two of his books had already been made into films (*Farewell, My Lovely* and *The Big Sleep*) but Ray had not been invited to work on the screenplays. He grumbled about that – as he did about a number of things that happened to him in Hollywood. Sometimes he did more than grumble.

I hardly knew Ray when he issued his first ultimatum to the studio. Typed on a long sheet of yellow paper, it listed the numerous indignities which he claimed he was suffering at the hands of his collaborator and demanded their instant redress. I remember two of his grievances. Item: Mr Wilder was at no time to swish under Mr Chandler's nose or to point in his direction the thin, leather-handled malacca cane which Mr Wilder was in the habit of waving around while they worked. Item: Mr Wilder was not to give Mr Chandler orders of an arbitrary or personal nature, such as 'Ray, will you open that window?' or 'Ray, will you shut that door, please?'

Apparently his demands were met, for he stayed on to finish the script. It was during this time that our friendship began, based on the surprising premise that he and I alone, of all those currently employed at Paramount, were British Public School Men – and, consequently, Gentlemen. It lasted till his death in 1959.

It is not always easy to remember that Chandler, whose literary territory was bounded by Malibu on the west, Long Beach on the south,

Chandler, age thirty, in the uniform of the
British Columbia Regiment at Seaford,
Sussex, where he had been sent from France
after everyone else in his outfit was wiped
out by German shells, 1918.

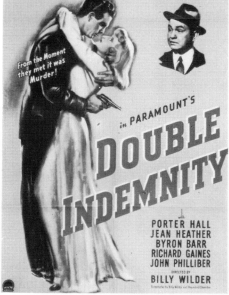

FRED
MacMURRAY ★ BARBARA
STANWYCK
EDWARD G. ROBINSON

From the Moment they met it was Murder!

in PARAMOUNT'S

DOUBLE INDEMNITY

PORTER HALL
JEAN HEATHER
BYRON BARR
RICHARD GAINES
JOHN PHILLIBER
DIRECTED BY
BILLY WILDER

OPPOSITE ABOVE: At a dinner for *Black Mask* writers in Los Angeles, 1936: left to right (*standing*) R.J. Moffat (a guest), Raymond Chandler, Herbert Stinson, Dwight Babcock, Eric Taylor, Dashiell Hammett; (*seated*) Arthur Barnes, John K. Butler, W.T. Ballard, Howard McCoy and Norbert Davis.
OPPOSITE BELOW: Hamish Hamilton jacket designs – the one on the right became a standard cover for British editions.
ABOVE: At Paramount in 1943 with Billy Wilder: 'Chandler said that all he ever knew about pictures was what he had learned from me. So there was a kind of resentment.'

ABOVE: Struggling with the script of *The Blue Dahlia*, 1945.

OPPOSITE: At the time they knew him: (*above left*) Dilys Powell, an early admirer of his work; (*above right*) Michael Gilbert, his British solicitor; (*below left*) Frank Norman, a protégé; and Natasha Spender, one of the friends who helped him when he was ill.

ALAN LADD
VERONICA LAKE
WILLIAM BENDIX

"THE BLUE DAHLIA"

a GEORGE MARSHALL production

HOWARD da SILVA · DORIS DOWLING · TOM POWERS · FRANK FAYLEN · A Paramount Picture

OPPOSITE: 'I had to hold Taki's tail to keep it still.' (La Jolla, 1948); BELOW: In London four years later.

ABOVE: Diving demonstration watched by Christopher Isherwood, California 1956.

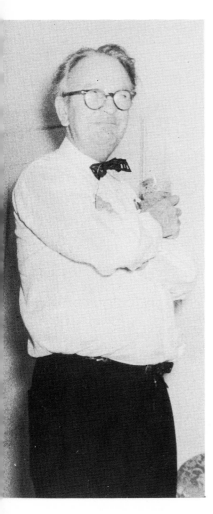

Before and after his cure, 1956.

and San Bernardino on the east, and whose writing gave the world some of its most ruthless documentation on the seamier aspects of Southern California society in the Twenties and Thirties of this century, had spent most of his adolescence in England and had been educated in the classics at Dulwich. When he appeared in my office at lunchtime, seeking relief from the pressures of the glib and forceful men with whom he was working, I think he was hoping to recapture with me, for a few moments, the sounds and memories of his childhood.

It was one of the basic inhibitions of that Public School system that you did not ask questions about your companion's past; consequently, I never got to know much about Chandler's life. There was a story around the studio that he had earned his living for a time stringing tennis rackets; there was also a rumour that he had, for many years, been an alcoholic. This was easy to believe, for the first impression Ray gave was one of extreme frailty; it was not till later that you discovered the peculiar strength that lay beneath his ashy, burnt-out look and his querulous hypochondria.

In life he was too inhibited to be gay; too emotional to be witty. And the English Public School system which he loved had left its sexually devastating mark upon him. The presence of young women – secretaries and extras around the lot – disturbed and excited him. His voice was normally muted; it was in a husky whisper that he uttered those juvenile obscenities at which he would have been the first to take offence, if they had been spoken by others.

Soon after he had finished *Double Indemnity* Ray came to work with me on what was to be my first film. Charles Brackett had just produced a successful ghost story called *The Uninvited*; what more natural than that the studio should change the title of my rather banal mystery to *The Unseen*? It was felt that the script needed some added toughness; who was more qualified to toughen a script than Ray Chandler? At a thousand dollars a week, Ray was agreeable. The fact that neither of us was under any delusion as to the transcendent merit of the project on which we were engaged helped to make the seven or eight weeks of our association relaxed and pleasant.

After the 'polish job' was over we continued to see each other occasionally. We dined together several times during the summer, and one Sunday afternoon Ray drove the monumental, grey-green, vintage Packard convertible of which he was so proud up the steep dirt road that ran around the edge of the hill between King's and Queen's Roads, high above Ciro's and the Hollywood Strip. From my terrace, to the right, we could see the Pacific and Catalina; far off to the left, still visible above the smog, the pyramidal tower of City Hall; directly below, the long thin line of La Cienega (before it became the Fifty-Seventh Street of the West) stretching directly ahead till it got lost among the oil wells of Baldwin Hills – all Chandler territory.

With him on these visits – with him, in fact, wherever he went, except to the studio – was his wife, Cissy. In Hollywood, where the selection of wives was frequently confused with the casting of motion pictures, Cissy was an anomaly and a phenomenon. Ray's life had been hard; he looked ten years older than his age. His wife looked twenty years older than he did and dressed thirty years younger. Later, after she had died, 'not by inches but by half-inches', Ray wrote to me of their 'thirty years, ten months and four days of as happy a marriage as any man could expect'.

He wrote from the loneliness of his big house overlooking the sea in La Jolla, where he and Cissy had hoped to retire. The letter ended:

Before I stop talking about myself – I don't really want to, but a lonely man does it too much, I know – I do like to remember what I worked on for you. We once wrote a picture called *The Blue Dahlia*, remember? It may not have been the best but at least we tried. And the circumstances *were* a bit difficult ...

I *do* remember. We *did* try. And the circumstances *were*, as Ray said, 'a bit difficult'.

It was early in 1945, not long after Buddy da Silva's stormy resignation, that the front office of the Paramount studio came to the horrifying realization that Alan Ladd, Paramount's top star and principal asset (at that time the highest-rated male performer in the US) would be re-entering the Army in three months' time, leaving behind him not one single foot for the company to release in his absence. At our next producers' meeting, between the dire threats and fulsome flatteries with which our new executive producer was wont to entertain us, we were given to understand that anyone coming up with an Alan Ladd vehicle ready to go into production within a month (a sheer impossibility) would earn the undying gratitude of the studio and of Mr Balaban, its chief stockholder.

Two days later Ray Chandler, lunching with me in one of the funereal cubicles at Lucey's, across the street from the studio, complained of being stuck on the book he was writing and muttered that he was seriously thinking of turning it into a screenplay for sale to the movies. After lunch, we went to his house – a small, Spanish-style stucco bungalow west of Fairfax, where Cissy was lying in a cloud of pink tarlatan, with a broken leg – and I read the first 120 typed pages of his book. Forty-eight hours later Paramount had bought *The Blue Dahlia* for a substantial sum and Ray Chandler was at work on a screen-play for Alan Ladd. I was to produce it, under the supervision of Joseph Sistrom, a lively second-generation Hollywood movie man who, with his pink cheeks and his stiff, black golliwog hair, looked like a schoolboy of fourteen.

In those lush days, it usually took about a year and a half to produce an A-picture. The average writing time for an adaptation was around five months; for an original, rather more. After that, there was a period of gestation to allow everybody to criticize and tamper with the script; this created the need for revisions which took another three months. Then came the casting. And while we had not yet reached the fantastic level of titanic negotiations that came later (as the business began to fall apart), it often took three or four months to find the right actors for a picture. Finally, a director having been chosen and having almost certainly demanded rewrites which might take another eight to fifteen weeks, production would start. The average shooting schedule for an A-picture was between seven and twelve weeks, and the editing and scoring took another three to four months after that.

Ray Chandler delivered the first half of his script – about forty-five minutes of film – in under three weeks, at the rate of four or five pages a day. This was no miracle; the scenes and the dialogue were already written, with transitions which Ray carried directly into the screen-play. After the first seventy pages had been mimeographed, a shooting date was set – three weeks away. Everyone was astounded, and busy taking credit.

Our director was one of the old maestros of Hollywood – George Marshall, who had been in movies since their earliest days, first as an actor, then as a director. He had never become one of the giants, but he held a solid and honourable position in the industry. His most famous picture was *Destry Rides Again*, which, according to him, he had practically created on the set. This and similar successes resulted in a state of mind (which he shared with many of his colleagues at the

57

time) in which the director showed absolutely no respect for the script and made it a point of prestige, justifying his high salary, to rewrite it almost entirely as he went along. It took a lot of earnest talk from me (though, since I was a beginner, George didn't pay much attention) and from Joe Sistrom to convince George Marshall that *The Blue Dahlia* was an inspired script which he was not expected to rewrite or improvise on the set.

Casting presented no serious problem. The leading part, as written by Chandler for Alan Ladd, was perfectly suited to the special qualities of that surprising star, who had played a part, so small that I barely remembered it, in *Citizen Kane* and had continued to work as a stage-hand, between jobs, until the lucky day on which he appeared in *This Gun for Hire*, playing a professional killer with a poignant and desolating ferocity that made him unique, for a time, among the male heroes of his day.

As a star, Ladd had some say in the choice of the persons with whom he worked. Since he himself was extremely short, he had only one standard by which he judged his fellow actors: their height. Meeting another actor for the first time, if his glance hit him or her anywhere below the collarbone, he was sure to explain as soon as we were alone that he didn't think he or she was exactly right for the part, and would we please find someone else.

Veronica Lake was the perfect size for him, but we had trouble over the part of his dissolute wife in which, not altogether perversely, we had cast a beautiful, dark-haired girl named Doris Dowling. Since she was a full half-foot taller than Ladd, he made a determined attempt to get rid of her; we placated him in their scenes together by keeping her sitting or lying down. Also in the cast were Bill Bendix and a whole troupe of those low-life types with whom motion pictures, and now television, have always been so plentifully populated.

Shooting of *The Blue Dahlia* went well from the start. By the end of our first week we were a day and a half ahead of schedule. In the next fortnight we gained another day. It was not until the middle of our fourth week that a faint chill of alarm invaded the studio when the script girl pointed out that the camera was rapidly gaining on the script. We had shot sixty-two pages in four weeks; Mr Chandler, during that time, had turned in only twenty-two – with another thirty to go.

Ray's problem with the script (as with the book) was a simple one: he had no ending. On page eighty-three of the shooting script he had reached the following *impasse*: Ladd's wife (all five foot seven of her) had been found shot – in a position that suggested, but clearly was not, suicide. Our hero was suspected (by the police, but not by anyone else) of having knocked her off in a rage on discovering the kind of life she had led during his absence in the South Pacific. Of the members of his bomber crew, with whom he had returned from the war, one was a dull and devoted friend; the other (Bill Bendix), who had a large silver plate in his head and convenient moments of total aberration, was under very serious suspicion which he was doing everything possible to aggravate. Obviously, he was innocent. There was a villain, lover of the hero's wife; as the main suspect he, too, was clearly above suspicion. There was also the villain's estranged wife (Veronica Lake), who had picked up our hero, at night, on the Pacific highway; but since she had immediately fallen in love with him and he with her – in a nice way – it was quite clear that the murder couldn't possibly be her work. Other characters and suspects included a professional killer, a number of petty crooks, two blackmailers, an ambulance chaser, a house detective, a bartender, and a night watchman, each of whom could very plausibly, with one or two added close-ups and a few planted lines, assume responsibility for the shooting.

Still, I was not worried. Ray had written such stories for years and I was quite confident that sooner or later (probably later since he seemed to enjoy the suspense) he would wind up the proceedings with an 'artistic' revelation (it was his word) and a caustic last line. But as the days went by and the camera went on chewing its way through the script and still no ending arrived, signs of tension began to appear. Joe Sistrom, who shared my faith in Ray but who was being tortured by the production department, called a couple of meetings in his quarters on the ground floor of the main Paramount office block, with its Elizabethan timbering and casement windows, to discuss the situation and to review our various suspects. And it was during one of these meetings, early one afternoon, that a man came running down the studio street, stopping at the various windows to shout something we could not hear to the people inside. When he reached us, he shoved his head in and told us that President Roosevelt was dead.

I remember that we sat stunned for a while. One by one, we said all the obvious things: how ill he had looked, already, on the photographs from Yalta; how reckless it had been of him to take that ride in the pouring rain through the New York streets; how he had looked and sounded on that morning of his first inauguration almost exactly twelve years ago – all the things that everyone was saying, in that moment, all over the world and would continue to say in the days and the years to come. Finally we fell silent and sat there gloomily for a while. Then, gradually, we drifted back to our story conference; half an hour later, we were deep in the intricacies of *The Blue Dahlia*, looking for the least likely suspect and trying to decide on whom it would be most satisfying to pin the murder. We went through all the tired alternatives, using them to smother the realities of the world outside, and Ray sat listening, only half there, nodding his head, saying little.

Two days later I was sitting in my office when my secretary hurried in to say that Mr Chandler was outside and was asking to see me. I was not used to this formality and there was something strange about the way she said it. When Ray came in, he was deadly pale and his hands were trembling. She made him a cup of coffee and, piece by piece, I heard his story: late the night before, Ray's agent had called him to say that the head of production would like to see him, privately, in his office, at nine-thirty the next morning. Ray spent a sleepless night; he was a timorous man and his agitation was increased by the admonition that he should, under no circumstances, mention the appointment to me.

When he appeared in the panelled executive office with the English hunting prints and the cream wall-to-wall carpet. Ray was told that the future of Paramount would be seriously imperilled if the balance of *The Blue Dahlia* script was not delivered on time. If it *was* – such would be the studio's gratitude and appreciation that a check for five thousand dollars would be exchanged, there and then, for the final page of script.

It was the front-office calculation, I suppose, that by dangling this fresh carrot before Chandler's nose they were executing a brilliant and cunning manœuvre. They did not know their man. They succeeded, instead, in disturbing him in three distinct and separate ways: one, his faith in himself was destroyed. By never letting Ray share my apprehensions, I had convinced him of my confidence in his ability to finish the script on time. This sense of security was now hopelessly shattered. Two, he had been insulted. To Ray, the bonus was nothing but a bribe. To be offered a large additional sum of money for the completion of an assignment for which he had already contracted and which he had every intention of fulfilling was by his standards a degradation and a dishonour. Three, he had been invited to betray a friend and fellow Public

School man. The way the interview had been conducted ('behind your back') filled Ray with humiliation and rage.

These accumulated grievances had reduced Ray to a state of nervous despair, the depth of which it took me some time to realize. But finally, when he assured me that his creative mechanism had been wrecked and that he had no choice but to withdraw from a project to which he had nothing more to contribute, I found myself believing him.

After he had gone – to lie down and, later, to discuss the matter with Cissy – I tried to evaluate my situation. The latest word from the sound stage was that we would complete page ninety-three before night. That left us with seven pages of unshot script plus two short scenes which we had delayed making till we knew who had done the killing. In all, less than three days' work. And in ten days' time Alan Ladd would vanish beyond hope of recovery into the US Army – forever.

The front office called in the afternoon over the executive intercom and I ignored the call. Joe Sistrom came around and I told him what had happened. While he was with me, we received from the sound stage what, in the circumstances, almost seemed like good news. During a scene of mayhem, one of our heavies had let a massive oak tabletop fall upon and break another heavy's toe. But when we reached the set, George Marshall told us not to worry; he had found a way for the injured heavy to play the rest of his scene from the floor. He also asked where the rest of the pages were.

The next morning, true to his promise, Chandler appeared in my office, looking less distraught but grimmer than the day before. He said that after a sleepless and tormented night he had come to the unalterable conclusion that he was incapable of finishing *The Blue Dahlia* script on time – or ever. This declaration was followed by a silence of several minutes during which we gazed at each other, more in sorrow than in anger. Then, having finished his coffee and carefully put down his cup on the floor, Ray spoke again, softly and seriously. After some prefatory remarks about our common background and the esteem and affection in which he held me, he made the following astonishing proposal: I was certainly aware (or had heard it rumoured) that he had for some years been a serious drinker – to the point where he had gravely endangered his health. By an intense effort of will he had managed to overcome his addiction. This abstinence, he explained, had been all the more difficult to sustain, since alcohol gave him an energy and a self-assurance that he could achieve in no other way. This brought us to the crux of the matter; having repeated that he was unable and unwilling to continue working on *The Blue Dahlia* at the studio, sober, Ray assured me of his complete confidence in his ability to finish it, at home – *drunk*.

He did not minimize the hazards: he pointed out that his plan, if adopted, would call for deep faith on my part and supreme courage on his, since he would in effect be completing the script at the risk of his life. (It wasn't the drinking that was dangerous, he explained, since he had a doctor who gave him such massive injections of glucose that he could last for weeks with no solid food at all. It was the sobering up that was perilous; the terrible strain of his return to normal living.) That was why Cissy had so long and so bitterly opposed his proposed scheme, till Ray had finally convinced her that honour came before safety, and that his honour was deeply engaged, through me, in *The Blue Dahlia*.

My first reaction was one of pure panic. Such is my own insecurity that contact with a human brain that is even slightly out of control frightens, repels, and finally enrages me. On that ground alone I was horrified by Ray's proposal. I also knew that if I was mad enough to take this risk, it would have to be entirely on my own responsibility and without the studio's knowledge. At this point Ray produced a sheet of yellow foolscap paper (of the same format as that on which he had drawn up Billy Wilder's ultimatum) and showed me the list of his basic logistical requirements:

A. Two Cadillac limousines, to stand day and night outside the house with drivers available for:
1. Fetching the doctor (Ray's or Cissy's or both).
2. Taking script pages to and from the studio.
3. Driving the maid to market.
4. Contingencies and emergencies.
B. Six secretaries – in three relays of two – to be in constant attendance and readiness, available at all times for dictation, typing, and other possible emergencies.
C. A direct line open at all times, to my office by day and the studio switchboard at night.

I took the paper from him and asked him for an hour to think it over. With great courtesy and understanding, Ray agreed. For half an hour I walked the studio streets. I visited the set where George informed me, not without satisfaction, that he'd be out of script by evening of the following day. I went to Sistrom's office by the back way. I showed him Ray's demands and told him I had decided to take the risk. Joe approved. He said if the picture closed down we'd all be fired anyway. He would give the front office some virus story and immediately requisition the limousines and the secretaries on different charge numbers.

I thanked him and went back down the hall to my office where Ray was sitting, reading *Variety*. With all the Public School fervour and *esprit de corps* that I could dredge up from the dim memory of my ten years at Clifton, I accepted his proposal.

Ray now became extremely happy and exhilarated. It was almost noon, and he suggested, as proof of my faith in him and of my confidence in the efficacy of our scheme, that we drive to the most expensive restaurant in Los Angeles and tie one on together immediately. We left the studio in Ray's open Packard and drove to Perino's where I watched him down three double martinis before eating a large and carefully selected lunch, followed by three double stingers. I then drove the Packard, with Ray in it, back to his house, where the two Cadillacs were already in position and the first relay of secretaries at their posts.

Early next morning the limousines were still there, shining in the sun. The drivers had been changed; so had the secretaries. Ray lay, passed out, on the sofa of his living room. On the table beside him was a tall, half-filled highball glass of bourbon; beside it were three typed pages of script, neatly corrected – Ray's work of the night. As one of the black limousines rushed me back to the studio, I learned what I should have guessed long ago: that the murderer of Doris Dowling was the house detective. Ray had given him a death scene:

The Blue Dahlia
(Save Film – and Win the War!)

NEWELL: Cheap, huh? Sure – a cigar and a drink and a couple of dirty bucks – that's all it takes to buy me! That's what *she* thought –
(*His voice suddenly grows hard and savage*)
Found out a little different, didn't she? Maybe I could get tired of being pushed around by cops – and hotel managers – and ritzy dames in bungalows. Maybe I could cost a little something. Just for once – even if I do end up on a slab.
(*He jerks a gun out of his pocket*)

Anybody want to go along with me? It's nice cool country. No offers, huh?

(*To Lloyd*)

All right, you! Get out of my way.

LLOYD: Sure – anything you say.

He puts his hand on the knob of the door. There is the sound of a gun shot. Newell staggers.

NEWELL: (*As he starts to collapse – keeping himself upright by an effort*) Just a minute, gentlemen – you got me – all – wrong . . .

As he falls –

DISSOLVE TO:

I was on the sound stage when a boy on a bicycle arrived with the pages, still damp from the mimeograph machines. George Marshall read them and found them acceptable, except for one scene where Ray had the heavy with the broken toe (which he hadn't heard about) still on his feet; but that was easily fixed. I think George had looked forward to saving the day by improvising the last week's work on the set, and that he was disappointed and perhaps a little hurt that we preferred the work of a man in an advanced stage of alcoholism to his own, but he behaved admirably. So did everyone else. The film was finished with six days to spare, and Alan Ladd went off to the Army, and Paramount made a lot of money.

During those last eight days of shooting Chandler did not draw one sober breath, nor did one speck of solid food pass his lips. He was polite and cheerful when I appeared and his doctor came twice a day to give him intravenous injections. The rest of the time, except when he was asleep, with his black cat by his side, Ray was never without a glass in his hand. He did not drink much. Having reached the euphoria that he needed, he continued to consume just enough bourbon and water to maintain him in that condition. He worked about a third of the time. Between eight and ten every evening, he sat in Cissy's room and they listened together to the Gas Company's programme of classical music on the radio. The rest of the time was spent in a light sleep from which he woke in full possession of his faculties and picked up exactly where he had stopped with whichever of the rotating secretaries happened to be with him. He continued until he felt himself growing drowsy again, then dropped back comfortably into sleep while the girl went into the next room, typed the pages, and left them on the table beside him to be reread and corrected when he woke up. As his last line of the script. Ray wrote in pencil: '*Did somebody say something about a drink of bourbon?*' – and that's how we shot it.

Ray had not exaggeráted when he said he was risking his life for *The Blue Dahlia*. His long starvation seriously weakened him and it took him almost a month to recover, during which his doctor came twice a day to administer mysterious and reviving shots which cost him a lot more than the 'bonus' he was to receive. During his convalescence he lay neatly dressed in fresh pyjamas under a silk robe; when I came to see him he would extend a white and trembling hand, and acknowledge my gratitude with the modest smile of a gravely wounded hero who had shown courage far beyond the call of duty.

In the years that followed we talked and wrote a lot about doing another movie or a television show together. It never happened. But we remained friends for thirteen years, even through a short period in which Ray pretended to be angry with me. I had written disparagingly, in *Vogue*'s annual 'American' issue, of the current Bogartian hero and bracketed him with Chandler's Philip Marlowe whom (paraphrasing Ray's own words) I described as a drab, melancholy man of limited intelligence and mediocre aspiration, who is satisfied to work for ten bucks a day and who, between drinks, gets beaten up regularly and laid occasionally. Ray wrote me a sharp letter in which he said that my piece was typical of the glib-thinking and crummy values that made him detest Hollywood producers and all their works. In his opinion, Marlowe and his kind were the last honest men left in our society; they did their assigned jobs and took their wages; they were not acquisitive nor did they rise in the world by stepping on other people's faces; they would never try to take over the earth nor would they compensate for their own weakness by pushing other people around. Marlowe's was, in fact, the only attitude that a self-respecting, decent man could maintain in today's rapacious and brutal world.

I did not see much of Ray after he went to live in La Jolla. And it was only in the last two years of his life, after Cissy was dead and Ray was travelling between La Jolla and London, that we once again began to exchange letters. It was in one of these that he wrote on a subject which, till then, I had always found him reluctant to discuss – his life as a writer:

What should a man do with whatever talent God happened in an absent moment to give him? Should he be tough and make a lot of money like me? Of course, you don't get it just by being tough. You lay your neck on the block in every negotiation. And for some reason unknown to me I still have my head. A writer has nothing to trade with but his life. And that's pretty hard when other people depend on you. So how much do you concede? I don't know. I could write a bestseller, but I never have. There was always something I couldn't leave out or something I had to put in. I don't know why ...

I am not a dedicated writer. I am only dedicated as a person ... Most writers are frustrated bastards with unhappy domestic lives. I was happy for too long a time, perhaps. I never really thought of what I wrote as anything more than a fire for Cissy to warm her hands at. She didn't even much like what I wrote. She never understood, and most people don't, that to get money you have to master the world you live in, to a certain extent, and not be too frail to accept its standards. And, also, they never understood that you go through hell to get money and then you use it mostly for other people who can't take the punishment but nevertheless have needs.

At the end, as a sort of postscript, he added:

I hope you know that I never thought of myself as important and never could. The word itself is even a bit distasteful. I have had a lot of fun with the American language; it has fascinating idioms, is constantly creative, very much like the English of Shakespeare's time, its slang and argot is wonderful, and so on. But I have lost Los Angeles. It is no longer the place I knew so well and was almost the first to put on paper. I have that feeling, not very unusual, that I helped create the town and was then pushed out of it by the operators. I can hardly find my way around any longer ...

Media Marlowes

PHILIP FRENCH

Except for the scarcely canonical *Playback* (which was worked up from a rejected screenplay), all of Raymond Chandler's novels have been filmed, one of them three times. In all a dozen actors have appeared as Philip Marlowe on the screen, radio and television, though the wireless and television scripts have been apocryphal works. These media Marlowes have come not single eyes, nor in battalions, rather, they have paraded in pairs.

First came the B-feature pseudo- or crypto-Marlowes, George Sanders and Lloyd Nolan in the early Forties. They were followed by two Thirties stars, Dick Powell and Humphrey Bogart, settling into middle-aged screen personas towards the end of World War II, in which like Chandler's shamus, they were exempted from military service despite their apparent fitness. The third pair were actors with little in common but the name Montgomery – Robert returning from the wars to re-establish his name, George seeking a professional identity independent of his wife, the singing star Dinah Shore. In their wake came two Hollywood character actors, Van Heflin and Gerald Mohr, lending only their voices as the Marlowes of the airwaves. Some years passed and the co-axial cable had connected America's East and West coasts before the television Marlowes arrived – the minor movie star of the Fifties Phil Carey in a short series for the small screen; the major television star of the Fifties James Garner in a full-scale picture for theatrical distribution. Finally in the self-conscious, nostalgia-ridden Seventies with the apotheosis of Chandler as a classic author and Marlowe as a legendary hero, two of the most charismatic stars left in Hollywood were trundled on stage as elegiac Marlowes – Elliott Gould, who was born the year *The Big Sleep* was published, and Robert Mitchum, who was drifting into an acting career when Chandler's first novel appeared.

During the time that Chandler was serving his literary apprenticeship as a *Black Mask* author and then establishing himself as a novelist in the early Forties, celluloid private eyes were almost as thick on the Hollywood studio floors as cowboys and more numerous than Bengal lancers or swashbucklers, those other adventure heroes of the period. Every company had a detective series or two on the conveyor belt – Philo Vance at Warner Brothers, William Crane and later Sherlock Holmes at Universal, the Falcon at RKO, Boston Blackie at Columbia, Charlie Chan, Mr Moto and Michael Shayne at Twentieth Century-Fox, and the most prestigious of all, the Thin Man series at MGM with William Powell and Myrna Loy as Dashiell Hammett's heavy-drinking, wise-cracking husband-and-wife team, Nick and Nora Charles. Except for the latter, which were still relatively modestly budgeted by MGM standards, all these pictures were produced rapidly on the cheap, and were voracious consumers of scripts. The first two movies based on Chandler novels were so much grist to these production mills. For a couple of thousand dollars, RKO acquired the movie rights to *Farewell, My Lovely* and transformed it into *The Falcon Takes Over* (1942), a vehicle for that smooth operator George Sanders as 'the Falcon', originally a creation of Michael Arlen's. The basic plot of Marlowe being hired by ex-convict Moose Malloy (Ward Bond) to find his vanished girl-friend Velma was maintained, and the *Monthly Film Bulletin* critic found that within the customary B-feature length of sixty-five minutes, 'all the ingredients of a reasonably good thriller are here', without noting its superior provenance. In that same year, 1942, Twentieth Century-Fox took *The High Window*, which they had purchased for a similarly low sum, and transformed it into the sixty-one minute Michael Shayne adventure *Time To Kill*, again sticking to the basic tale of the detective being hired by the vicious old Mrs Murdock (played by the veteran British character actress Ethel Griffies) to recover a rare coin stolen from her collection. Lloyd Nolan played Brett Halliday's sleuth Shayne (he later appeared as the crooked Bay City police lieutenant in *The Lady in the Lake*), and the *Monthly Film Bulletin* reviewer, once again failing to note the source, reported that the picture was 'well produced and full of action, but the story is at times involved and difficult to follow.' Similar comments would be made about most of the subsequent films.

Meanwhile, however, over at other major studios things were stirring. In 1941, Warner Brothers decided to make a Grade-A movie of Dashiell Hammett's *The Maltese Falcon* (previously filmed in 1931 and 1936) starring Humphrey Bogart, more or less on the right side of the law for a change, as Sam Spade. The result was an enormous success, both critically and commercially, something the company had not anticipated, for Bogart returned to the other side of the social tracks to play a couple of low-life characters in his next two pictures. The following year Raymond Chandler, who had settled in California shortly before Cecil B. De Mille arrived in Hollywood to lay the foundations for what became Paramount Studios, was invited by Paramount to adapt James M. Cain's hard-boiled novel *Double Indemnity* with its director Billy Wilder. The immense success in 1943 of this black thriller coupled with the continuing popularity of *The Maltese Falcon* clearly suggested a remake of *Farewell, My Lovely* to RKO and influenced Warner Brothers' decision to acquire the rights to Chandler's *The Big Sleep*.

Dick Powell was forty and still trying to shake off the boyish romantic image his 1930s musicals at Warner Brothers had established when he persuaded RKO to cast him as Marlowe in *Farewell, My Lovely*. Under the direction of Edward Dmytryk (who was bent on making something special of his first major movie), Powell decisively altered the direction of his career, passing through the film absorbing punishment with the imperturbability of a punchbag, handing out wisecracks from a grim, frequently unshaven face, with only a certain grace of movement (which for a few seconds breaks out into a couple of parodic dance-steps in his client's vast reception hall) to remind us of his earlier films. Some, including myself, are still tempted to award the palm to this first screen Marlowe. At the last minute the company had cold feet about the title; when previews suggested that audiences might think they were in for a Dick Powell musical comedy, RKO released the picture as *Murder My Sweet*, though the original title was kept for Great Britain where Chandler's literary reputation stood higher.

Murder My Sweet is told in flashback by Marlowe to the cops, with a stylish running commentary that incorporates a good deal of the original narrative in a convincing pastiche. The only major concessions to the movies in John Paxton's script are a clarification of the plot and the omission of specific charges of police corruption.* The picture has all the key elements of the classic Forties *film noir* – the expressionist use of shadows, silhouettes and oddly disconcerting camera angles that Hollywood imported from the German cinema along with many of its major artists and technicians; the dark wet streets of the menacing night city; the sleazy hotels, garish bars and flashy night clubs; the spoilt rich shelling out fortunes to protect their family skeletons; the brutal suspicious police; the beautiful treacherous women (with Claire Trevor as Velma/Mrs Grail playing one of the screen's most unforgettable *femmes fatales*); the shadowy supporting cast of gamblers, blackmailers, drug-pushers, phoney therapists who blink with terror whenever they move out of their twilight world into the sunshine; the pervasive sense of an almost universal corruption. RKO came to specialize for a while in this type of picture and Dmytryk was able to draw on the neo-expressionist

* Stephen Pendo's book *Raymond Chandler On Screen* (Metuchen. The Scarecrow Press. 1976) contains a detailed analysis of the differences between Chandler's novels and the movie versions.

vocabulary recently established at the studio by Orson Welles' *Citizen Kane* and Val Lewton's horror films.

Though also begun in 1944, *The Big Sleep* was not released until 1946, and its Marlowe, Humphrey Bogart, was again much shorter than Chandler's ideal six-footer – a subject actually made a joke of in the first reel. Nevertheless, for many, Bogart's cool, fast-talking knight errant is the definitive impersonation, though others feel that it is too little differentiated from other similar roles. If Howard Hawks' version of *To Have and Have Not* (1944) started out to reprise *Casablanca*, *The Big Sleep* set out to exploit the Bogart–Lauren Bacall relationship established in *To Have and Have Not*, and it is their brilliantly comic, romantic teamwork that makes this an altogether more genial, less bitter experience than *Murder My Sweet*. The film's central erotic motif is the pair of smouldering cigarettes lying together in an ashtray against which the credit titles are shown.

Like Dmytryk's picture, Hawks's was shot entirely in the studio and the settings are largely nocturnal. But characteristically, Hawks eschewed unusual angles or excessively stylized lighting, and in order to focus our attention evenly upon Bogart and Bacall, he shoots their conversations with both of them in the frame, that is as a series of two-shots. Unlike *Murder My Sweet*, *The Big Sleep* makes little attempt to clarify the book's storyline, and at one point Hawks and his screenwriters Leigh Brackett and William Faulkner phoned Chandler to discover who had actually murdered General Sternwood's chauffeur. He was not able to enlighten them and they gave up worrying. But audiences (if not critics) didn't bother about the labyrinthine plot or the unexplained loose ends. Indeed the cult that has grown up around this film is believed to have contributed to the modern lack of interest in coherent narration, logical plot development and well-constructed screenplays. Nevertheless, the film takes most of its plot and much of its best dialogue from Chandler, and the picture was actually advertised with a trailer showing Bogart going into a bookstore and asking for 'a good mystery like *The Maltese Falcon*', and being given what is somewhat misleadingly described as 'Raymond Chandler's latest' by a girl assistant, who says: 'What a picture that'll make!'

Before *The Big Sleep* was released, Raymond Chandler spent several months at MGM adapting *The Lady in the Lake* for the screen, his only attempt at a movie version of one of his own novels, and he eventually abandoned it to Steve Fisher, a writer of no particular distinction who nevertheless wrote a few interesting crime pictures in the Forties. The most significant change in the adaptation is to have Marlowe infinitely more depressed and disillusioned than in the book, and living in a crummy hotel rather than having an apartment of his own. Instead of being hired by a cosmetics manufacturer to find his missing wife, he's engaged to work for the boss of a pulp publishing house to which he has submitted a detective story that he hopes might take him out of private investigation into authorship. This change parallels Chandler's own switch from business to writing and might be taken also as reflecting Chandler's own mixed feelings about being distracted from the serious business of writing fiction by the frivolous but highly paid activity of churning out screenplays.

Fisher took a single credit on the film when Chandler refused to have his name associated with the result, which turned out to be highly successful at the box office, the third Chandler hit on the run. But the abiding interest in this film resides in actor–director Robert Montgomery's decision to shoot the picture using a subjective camera throughout. Except for an opening sequence in which Marlowe (who in this instance spells his Christian name with two LS) speaks directly to the audience, we only see him when his face is reflected in a mirror. Otherwise we, the audience, *are* the detective. As we're told at the beginning: 'You'll see it just as I saw it. You'll meet the people; you'll find the clues. And maybe you'll solve it quick and maybe you won't.' This technique, however is only suited to brief sequences or occasional shots. One's visual perception of the world is quite different to that of the movie camera, and for all the technical ingenuity involved in making the picture, the result is slow, lumbering and self-conscious. As for Robert Montgomery, one might think him the closest screen Marlowe in style and appearance to Chandler's professed ideal, Cary Grant. He is tall, debonair, carefully groomed, conventionally handsome and with a gift for light comedy. Yet in this film he came over as wooden, whining, and altogether too sleek for the downbeat characterization of the script. Montgomery, nonetheless, went on to direct himself in several more films, without ever establishing a reputation as a director. Eventually he drifted from acting into Republican politics.

The Lady in the Lake is overrated, but still fairly entertaining, and the credit titles contain a charming joke in listing the dead Chrystal Kingsley as being played by one Ellay Mort (i.e. *elle est morte*). On the other hand, the second version of *The High Window* (1947) is underrated, to the extent that it is invariably dismissed out of hand. Shown in America as *The Brasher Doubloon* (though, like *Murder My Sweet*, retaining the novel's title in Britain) this movie was something less than a major Twentieth Century-Fox production, just as the handsome ex-boxer George Montgomery was something less than a major star. He is the only Marlowe with a moustache and the first to smoke a pipe.

The picture was directed by John Brahm, who served his apprentice-ship in Europe, and his Chandler assignment was preceded by several admirable minor *films noirs*, most notably the two period pieces *The Lodger* (from Mrs Belloc Lowndes' novel) and *Hangover Square* (derived somewhat remotely from Patrick Hamilton). Brahm charged the open-ing half-hour of a fairly short (seventy-two minute) picture with con-siderable atmosphere, and *The Brasher Doubloon* always looks good, if rather self-consciously so. The fine German actor Fritz Kortner turned in a striking performance as the blackmailer Vannier, as did Florence Bates as his unpleasant victim, Mrs Murdock. The script however, which used the by then conventional tough-guy commentary, is fairly ordinary and George Montgomery, though by no means lacking in pre-sence, is wholly lacking in depth and has little true individuality.

The Brasher Doubloon was released in May 1947 and some twenty-two years elapsed before another Marlowe appeared on the big screen. In 1947, however, Marlowe at last joined Sam Spade among the radio sleuths, with Van Heflin, a rising character actor on his way to minor stardom, in the lead. The short, crumple-faced Heflin bore no physical resemblance to any possible Marlowe, and at the end of the summer season his studio, MGM, refused to let him continue.

The following year *The Adventures of Philip Marlowe* took to the air again, this time with the thick-set 'heavy', Gerald Mohr, as Marlowe. (Mohr was then appearing on the screen as the hero of Columbia's B-feature 'Lone Wolf' detective series.) The original scripts owed little to Chandler beyond the general wise-cracking hard-boiled style of narra-tion. The series ran for two years, over a hundred shows, and returned in the summer of 1951, with Mohr still in the lead, for a further run of three months, after which it was dropped for good. Chandler had no connection with the production or scripting of any of these shows, but professed himself moderately pleased with Mohr's performance.

From the early 1950s there was talk about a television Marlowe, but apart from an appearance by Dick Powell in a small screen version of *The Long Goodbye* that launched a series called *Climax* in 1954, there was no Marlowe series until after Chandler's death. In 1959 Phil Carey was cast in an ABC network series which lasted just one quarter and was broadcast early in 1960 by the BBC (on Monday evenings in the peak time between *This Is Your Life* and *Panorama*) to widespread derision. The bland, vacuously handsome Carey, veteran good guy of numerous minor Westerns and war movies, was equipped with a smart open-plan apartment overlooking the harbour at Newport Beach where he had a cabin cruiser to help in his professional and amorous activities. The affluence did not sit well on Chandler's down-at-heel puritan, and the nautical aspect suggested that the adaptors had perhaps confused him with another perennial investigator, Conrad's Marlow. Certainly this one played by Carey was almost indistinguishable from the other homogenized private operatives packing their cases into half an hour (minus five minutes for commercials) that were then clogging the airways – the long-forgotten Peter Gunn, for instance, the equally unmemorable Johnny Staccato and the well-heeled denizens of *77 Sunset Strip.* The departure of the television Marlowe after some thirteen episodes was unlamented and he soon faded into oblivion. Very few absent television heroes are recalled with affection. One who is, is the tongue-in-cheek, mildly anti-heroic frontier gambler, Brett Maverick, a role that brought fame to James Garner and led to him transferring to the big screen.

During the 1960s, espionage agents dominated the cinema and television screens; James Bond led the field together with the *Men From UNCLE*, Derek Flint, Matt Helm and other *Playboy* heroes of the Western world in hot pursuit. However, a successful screen version of Ross MacDonald's *The Moving Target* (1966) with Paul Newman as the Chandleresque Los Angeles sleuth Lew Harper (changed from the novel's Lew Archer because Newman wanted another 'H' in his run of successes with *The Hustler, Hud* and *Hombre* – the film's American title is *Harper*), was followed by Frank Sinatra as the Miami-based gumshoe Tony Rome in *Tony Rome* (1967) and *Lady in Cement* (1968), two pictures that bear a suspiciously close resemblance to Chandler in character and plot. And this persuaded MGM that the time was ripe for a film version of *The Little Sister.* Adapted in workaday fashion by Sterling Silliphant and updated from Chandler's movie – Hollywood to the television-dominated film colony of 1969 – the picture was called simply *Marlowe* and starred James Garner. *Marlowe* was directed as his first feature film by a television hand, Paul Bogart, and he brought little flair to the task. Marlowe was equipped with a nubile mistress and on-going sex-life and, shades of things to come, the martial arts expert Bruce Lee was brought in to wreck the detective's office and deliver a few kicks and chops to Marlowe himself. The result was commonplace stuff with James Garner strolling amiably through the film exuding wry defensive charm. A few years later he was doing much the same thing back on television with his own private detective series *The Rockford Files*. Like George Montgomery he smoked a pipe, but he was the first screen Marlowe to go hatless and that absence of the snap-brimmed fedora was a sign of changing times. *Marlowe* was also the first Chandler adaptation in colour, and that too made a big change from the old black-and-white, once thought essential for urban thrillers, and it was the first to make extensive use of genuine Los Angeles locations, though these were not exploited in any significant fashion. Altogether the film seemed less authentically Chandlerian than did *The Moving Target* which like many subsequent private eye pictures contained conscious references or homages to earlier films. It opens for instance with Paul Newman being hired by a wheelchair-ridden millionaire living in hot-house luxury, just as Marlowe was at the beginning of *The Big Sleep* by General Sternwood. However, the crippled millionaire in *The Moving Target* is played by Lauren Bacall, the actress who appeared as Sternwood's amorous daughter in the Chandler movie.

On the face of it, the next screen Marlowe, Elliott Gould in Robert Altman's *The Long Goodbye* (1973), has more in common with his immediate predecessor, Garner, than with his successor, Robert Mitchum, in director Dick Richards' fastidious remake of *Farewell, My Lovely* (1975). Like Garner, Gould is a youngish man who established his reputation as a comedian, and his Marlowe, like Garner's, goes around present-day Los Angeles hatless and meeting the world with a nonchalant, nervously smiling air. Mitchum on the other hand is the nearest thing possible to Powell and Bogart; indeed, he is the prime survivor of their generation and a product of the very RKO studio that launched the screen career of Chandler's private eye. He acted in numerous *films noirs*, including ones directed by John Brahm (*The Locket*, 1946) and Edward Dmytryk (*Crossfire*, 1947), and appeared as a doomed private investigator in a classic crime thriller, Jacques Tourneur's *Build My Gallows High* (1947, shown in the US as *Out of the Past*). Moreover, Mitchum is an authentic Forties Marlowe in a literal sense, going down the mean streets of Los Angeles in the summer of 1941, a Camel between his lips and a wide-brimmed hat on his head or being played through his fingers.

Yet these two Marlowes and the minor masterpieces in which they figure resemble each other quite closely. *Farewell, My Lovely* is an account of the Forties in terms of the present; *The Long Goodbye* is an account of the present in terms of the Forties. Altman's perennial subject is the defeat or ambiguous triumph of the inner-directed man in a greedy other-directed society, and it is also a recurrent theme in Chandler and the one taken up by Dick Richards and his screenwriter David Zelag Goodman. There is, technically, another major factor linking these movies, establishing a shared tone and defining their character. Both were shot entirely on location, which in the case of *Farewell, My Lovely* meant hunting down and then dressing up some striking remnants of the old Los Angeles. In order to secure the particularly muted pastel-shades that Altman sought, his cameraman Vilmos Zsigmond experimented with 'post-flashing' (i.e. exposing the negative to further light before development) to give the images a strange, distanced look, suggesting that the film, though not actually set in the past, was somehow a memory or echo of a distant time. In the case of *Farewell, My Lovely* the producers engaged the set designer Dean Tavoularis (who had been responsible for the *Godfather* films) and cameraman John A. Alonzo (who worked on Polanski's *Chinatown*, set in 1937 Los Angeles), and they used the Japanese film stock Fujicolor (the first major Hollywood film to do so) to secure a similar kind of pastel effect, in this case a hazy, dreamlike sensation to suggest a period in the past but not yet beyond recall. Inevitably this elegiac patina is far more pronounced in *Farewell, My Lovely* than in *The Long Goodbye*.

By the time these two films were made the last censorship barriers had fallen in Hollywood, so both directors were free to include much profanity, explicit references to homosexuality, the obligatory nudity, open acknowledgement of police corruption and brutality, and to be simultaneously franker and more liberal on matters of race. Yet in the midst of this permissiveness, neither Mitchum nor Gould goes to bed with anyone, though temptation is frequently thrown in their way. They are both solitary mysogynists, almost too lethargic one might think for prolonged sexual activity, and – in choosing males as companions and confidants – fitting a pattern of movie heroes in the Seventies. Whereas earlier adaptors have been forced to inject romantic interest into Marlowe's life, here it is left out or, in the case of *The Long Goodbye* where the book's Marlowe actually did go to bed with Linda Loring, eliminated.

Though Robert Altman is as confused and romantic as Chandler, his

76

film (scripted by Leigh Brackett, co-screenwriter on *The Big Sleep*) removed the crutches on which Marlowe survived in the novel: by updating the action he eliminates the World War II experiences that bind the characters together, and secondly, by turning Marlowe's friend Terry Lennox into a coldly calculating murderer instead of a suspected killer he destroys the basis of faith and comradeship that provided the moral and narrative spine of the book, as well as casting doubt upon Marlowe's powers of judgment. Yet Altman's Southern California is not as far removed from Chandler's as has been made out – it is merely that the corruption and decadence are now more on the surface. Pornography, for instance, is today sold openly on Hollywood Boulevard and not peddled, as in *The Big Sleep* days, in the backroom of phoney rare bookshops. The characters are obsessed with the recent past, or its pop cultural manifestations: Marlowe and Lennox play trivia quiz games; a dog blocking Marlowe's old car is referred to as 'Asta' (name of the Thin Man's pet); the gatekeeper at an odiously luxurious private housing estate forces visitors to guess which Hollywood stars he is impersonating (his repertoire includes Cary Grant, whom we know of course to be Chandler's ideal Marlowe, and Barbara Stanwyck in a scene Chandler wrote for *Double Indemnity*) and so on. And quite deliberately Altman has cast the picture to set up weird resonances, so that no one in this hallucinatory town is quite what he or she seems. Thus the *femme fatale* Eileen Wade is played by Nina van Pallandt, a singer and, through her association with Clifford Irving during the Hughes autobiography scandal, an international celebrity. As her hard-drinking Hemingway-esque husband we have Sterling Hayden, a 'friendly witness' before the House Un-American Activities Committee who loathes his Hollywood past and now regards himself as a writer. The bland *Laugh-In* comic Henry Gibson appears as the sinister epicene sanitorium owner. Jim Bouton, a baseball star turned author makes his movie debut as Lennox. Almost the only full-time professional actor around is Elliott Gould, who is virtually the antithesis of the earnest, confident, WASPish Marlowes of the past, and he drifts somnambulistically through the proceedings, very much not in control as narrator or shaper: no existential hero he, more a victim in fact. Gould chain-smokes not like the casual 1940s stars but rather as if he were a cigarette-puffing machine in a cancer research clinic. As everyone knows, both Humphrey Bogart and Dick Powell died of cancer, but neither acted at the time as if they had some kind of overpowering death wish.

At the end Marlowe sets aside his diffidence and acts with sudden positive assertion – by killing Terry Lennox in the swimming pool of his Mexican hideaway. Then he ambles happily away down a country road to the sound of a scratchy record of 'Hooray for Hollywood' (from the old 1937 Dick Powell musical *Hollywood Hotel*). He is liberated from the mean streets of Los Angeles, and by implication from the world of the *film noir*, for there is a clear reference here to the concluding sequence of the ultimate in doomed Forties movies, *The Third Man*, treated by Altman as comedy with a hero happy and mobile, instead of depressed, inert and rejected, after the second (and real) death of a treacherous friend.

More liberties have been taken with the plot of *The Long Goodbye* than with any other adaptation, but the controversy that has surrounded Altman's alleged iconoclasm, inviting praise and blame in equal measure, has obscured the fact that the movie is essentially faithful to the spirit of Chandler and paradoxically far more optimistic in tone than the novel seemed back in 1954.

If *The Long Goodbye* was intended to be anti-nostalgic, *Farewell, My Lovely* is a product of the nostalgia boom, following in the wake of *The Sting*, *The Great Gatsby*, *Chinatown* and other films romantically re-creating the America of the inter-war years. Los Angeles is lovingly observed in all its sleazy glory, and some of the nostalgia is a chic kind of *nostalgie de la boue*. The sordid hotel room with its garish neon sign outside the window in which Marlowe meets Lieutenant Nulty to tell him the story in flashback; the smoky dance hall with a blowzy *chanteuse* belting out 'It seems I've heard that song before' where Marlowe goes at the beginning to find a client's runaway daughter; the run-down black night-club where Moose Malloy drags Marlowe in search of Velma; Jessie Florian's decrepit Spanish-style stucco house; the plush brothel mansion of Florence Amthor (the film's lesbian conflation of the novel's phoney Dr Sonderborg and psychic consultant Jules Amthor); Laird Brunette's gambling ship (for which the *Queen Mary* at Long Beach was used) – all these places are hauntingly evoked, and are more important than details of plot or the business of detection.

As *Farewell, My Lovely* begins, Marlowe tells Nulty and us that he is tired out and at the end of his tether, and the chain-smoking Mitchum, for all that he still moves like a sleepy panther, looks old now, his face lined, heavy bags beneath his hooded eyes. (Mitchum was in fact, at fifty-eight, the oldest actor to play Marlowe, though he was born in 1917, the year after the screen's youngest Marlowe, George Montgomery.) As he searches for Velma, Marlowe follows the record-breaking fifty-six-game winning streak of Joe Di Maggio through the summer and autumn of 1941, more interested in that than the newspapers' other front-page stories about the progress of the war in Europe. (In Altman's *Long Goodbye*, Marlowe and Lennox challenge each other just to recall the names of the Di Maggio brothers.) At the end it is late autumn and Marlowe stands playing with a pin-ball baseball game in a dreary amusement arcade, deserted except for a soldier and his girlfriend. Marlowe has solved his case leaving all three of his clients dead, Di Maggio's unbroken series of safe games has come to an end, America is about to go to war. A world with its set of values, its heroes and its peculiar customs has drawn to a close, the film says, though never defining precisely which world, and we have been watching its final entropic movements as it winds inexorably down, watching it as in a peep show or through the wrong end of a telescope.

This elegiac movie is one of the best Marlowe pictures, a thriller of mood and character rather than suspense or excitement, and with at its centre an assured performance by Robert Mitchum that is without self-pity but charged with selfconscious melancholy. Where *The Long Goodbye* is a chilly critical analysis of Chandler's work and the private eye genre, *Farewell, My Lovely* is a warmly affectionate meditation on the form and the world of its pre-eminent exponent. After this there is no immediate need for another version, and the picture establishes the extent to which Marlowe – if not necessarily his values and ethical code – belongs to a time that has now passed.

Ray and Cissy

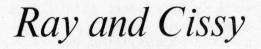

DILYS POWELL

Memo to self: Keep diary in book with large pages, write clearly in ink on non-absorbent paper.

Reconstructing the past, I struggle with minuscule records. I must have used the pencil from the tube at the back of the pocket diary; it was never sharpened, the writing is indecipherable. Sometimes I have scribbled to clarify, but the ink has soaked through, blotting both sides of the wafer-paper. I strain, I peer through a magnifying-glass; now I understand the toil of the scholar battling to recover the text erased by fire, earthquake, tidal wave. A word or two. 'Cold', I make out; then something which looks like 'influenza'. And a name. Can it be Cissy? I don't know anybody called Cissy. Whom could I be referring to in my diary for 1952?

With the date memory clears. Cissy is Cissy Chandler, that frail enigma of a wife on whom Raymond Chandler conferred something of his own celebrity. By 1952 I had enjoyed a long acquaintance with Raymond Chandler – long and remote. It began some time late in the war. Autumn: I know it was autumn, for I had a cold; I always used to get a cold in autumn. I needed distraction, and as my husband Leonard Russell – he was literary editor of the *Sunday Times* – was setting off for the office, 'Could you,' I said, 'bring me a thriller?' I was still an addict of the British detective story, the British thriller. I still puzzled over the storm-bound house-party and the guests picked off one by one, or the escape from the guarded, locked, windowless room with the door Scotch-taped on the outside. When Leonard came home he handed me a book. 'I think,' he said, 'you ought to have a look at this man Chandler.' It was called *The Big Sleep*. American: not what I had expected. I had not yet taken to the American novel of crime. I had seen John Huston's film of *The Maltese Falcon*, but I had never read Dashiell Hammett. The cinema, I felt, not the printed word, was the proper vehicle for transatlantic murder. Gloomily breathing through my mouth – I really had a terrible cold – I began to read.

An unsatisfactory start. No body, no house-party or Scotch tape, no suspects, no clues, no deft interrogations. True, there was a detective of sorts: Marlowe. But he set about his job in a highly unorthodox fashion. I sneezed and read on. There was something, certainly there was something about the writing. I should never have believed in Marlowe if he had existed in a description by the author. But this was an 'I' character, insolent, self-explanatory, self-sufficient. His actions described him; one accepted him as one accepted the society, glossy or grainy, into which detection took him. And the setting: car lights in the Californian rain, the dark banked canyons, a powerful undertow of sex – a miasma of corruption, a whisky-breath hung over the scene. And the action: blackmail, drugs, bullets – for now things began to happen, savagely, disjointedly. Difficult to follow, impossible to understand the sequence of events. But did it matter? What mattered was the sense of the city, a squirming underworld, the sardonic, resourceful figure of Marlowe. Sweating, I read on. It wasn't my cold which made me sweat. I was high on Chandler.

Perhaps *The Big Sleep* was the best of the Chandler books. I think it was. Perhaps one grew accustomed to Marlowe's ironic rejoinders, to the narrative ferocity. That first shock was not repeated. Nevertheless the pleasure persisted. 'Isn't there another Chandler?' I would say to Leonard. Together we began to look out for the new Marlowe stories, just as a hundred years ago one might have looked out for a new instalment of some stirring Victorian novel. We read *Farewell, My Lovely* and *The High Window* and, as time went on, *The Lady in the Lake* and *The Little Sister*. Presently I noticed the name of Chandler in the credits of the films I was then reviewing. He had collaborated, I found, with Billy Wilder on the script of *Double Indemnity*. Delighted to share what at the time seemed a discovery, I took the opportunity of writing something about his printed work, his depiction of a society of Bourbon breakfasts and encounters in dingy bedrooms, roadhouses, petrol stations, shacks on half-made roads.

In the following year there came the first film to do anything like justice to a Chandler novel: *Farewell, My Lovely*. There had, I found, been an earlier version. *The Falcon Takes Over*, it was called. George Sanders played the Falcon, and according to those who had seen it the piece bore only minimal resemblances to its original. Even now Chandler did not write his own script; the job was done by John Paxton. But it was honourably done. It was recognizable, I said, as a serious attempt at translating to the cinema the Chandler mixture of high polish and back-street poetry. I am glad I said poetry, for a kind of shady poetry is indeed there in that airless underworld.

English readers were beginning to appreciate not only the excitement of the fast-moving action but the quality of the prose. Possibly the American public was too close to its own scene to enjoy the translation into the raffish world of Chandler. At any rate in his own country he was not yet taken seriously. Towards the end of the war Leonard and

I met some of the American literary figures who, disguised as members of the armed forces, were arriving in London. Among them were Irwin Shaw and William Saroyan; we invited them to have a drink with us at the Café Royal. We met, we talked, we discussed the qualities of American fiction.

'And,' I said, 'you have Raymond Chandler.'

'Chandler!' they exclaimed, almost in unison. 'A pulp writer!' And they looked at me pityingly. It was as if I had advanced Mickey Spillane as a candidate for the Nobel Prize.

I dare say this lack of recognition made Chandler welcome his English reviews. At any rate it was about this time that our acquaintance ripened into misunderstanding. Desmond MacCarthy was then chief literary critic of the *Sunday Times*; Leonard edited the literary pages. Amalgamating the two functions, Chandler wrote to a correspondent in England. He was, he said glad of the appreciation of a lady called Dilys Powell who was, he believed, the wife of Desmond MacCarthy. We on our side had by now sorted out the Chandler relationship. We knew nothing about Cissy, but we had heard of her. It was still some time before we were to meet. But at last we learned that the pair of them were coming to England. It was 1952. We had emerged from the austerities of the war, London was beginning to look like itself; people gave parties for distinguished visitors. Leonard wrote to Raymond to ask him and Cissy to dinner. Raymond ('yours very truly') accepted in his looped, trailing hand. No dressing, he wrote, he took to mean no black tie. Or no white tie? He hadn't got one anyway. The interview, he added (Leonard had fixed up something for the *Sunday Times*), had gone off in 'a cloud of brandy fumes'. Later he said that the photographic records had got mixed and that the paper had printed a picture not of him but of Grandma Moses ...

What we expected of the Chandlers I don't know, but I can still see their arrival in our house: Raymond stocky, middle-aged, in glasses – I have the impression of the colour brown; just as with Cissy I associate a pale, almost an extinct canary colour. Among our guests were Nick Bentley, himself a thriller writer and son of E.C. Bentley of *Trent's Last Case*, and his wife, daughter of the famous QC Sir Patrick Hastings; Val Gielgud was with us, and so were the late Campbell Dixon and his wife; Campbell, film critic of the *Daily Telegraph*, thought Chandler inferior to Jonathan Latimer, a friend and neighbour of Raymond's, but kept it to himself.

At first Raymond seemed a little on the defensive. There was in his manner, friendly though it was, a tinge of the suspicion which Americans used to feel of the English. The fact that he had been educated in England may have sharpened his sensibilities; from his knowledge of the people of this country half a century earlier, he may have retained the idea that we might be high-hatted. Or more likely he was defensive on behalf of Cissy, sitting next to Leonard at the other end of the table. I have been quoted as saying that she was older than her husband. So she was, but I was speaking out of hindsight. I didn't that evening notice her age, and it was only when our guests had left and Leonard commented that I thought about it. At dinner I now and then looked to see how she was getting on. Conversation flowed round her: about California, the cops, Raymond's work. She appeared to be taking a modest part in it; and leaning amiably towards Leonard, she smiled and listened.

At last Raymond had his chance. Feeling it was time to leave the men to their drinks. I tried to catch Cissy's eye. No luck. I tried again. Still no luck. Then Raymond, who had been watching with amusement, stood up. 'Cissy!' he cried. 'Cissy, look at this!' And he clapped his hands. 'An old English custom,' he added as we shambled out. He was delighted with himself. And I believe the evening, 'alcoholic', in his words, 'as it was', really gave him pleasure; he said it did in one of his letters from America. Perhaps we were less formal than he had feared; he could drop his defences. And he had scored off my modest exercise in ceremony. Not that he was without his own brand of the formal. In letters to Leonard (he never corresponded with me while Cissy was alive) he would refer to me as Dilys Powell. It took him years to get round to Dilys.

A few days later we were invited to have drinks with the Chandlers. They were staying at the Connaught: 'a couple of pink gins' was his description of the entertainment. Neither Raymond nor Cissy looked entirely at ease in the hotel, chic haunt of eminent transatlantic visitors. But we were friends. He didn't need, now, to defend Cissy, only to watch over her. Looking at her then, I could see the creases in the pale face. But she still managed to be a pretty woman. The features small, neat, regular, the faded hair fluffy, dressed, as it must have been dressed when he first knew her, in the fashion of the 1920s – a vestigial feminine charm still lingered. The manner was gentle, sweet; she still smiled, still leaned to listen, watchfully took her drink. What did she talk about? Nothing: one heard only the exchanges of polite society. But I thought I detected in her something propitiatory – propitiatory for her age, her physical frailty, the gradual extinction of her energy.

A few weeks later the Chandlers went back to the United States. We never saw her again. From their American home at the end of the year Raymond, wishing us for Christmas 'whatever in this sad world remains of peace and happiness', wrote that she had been very ill. Two years later she was dead.

Leonard wrote to him; his response has been quoted in Frank Mac-Shane's *The Life of Raymond Chandler*. 'She was,' he said, 'the beat of my heart for thirty years. She was the music heard faintly at the edge of sound.' In his misery he was turning, as a writer will, to the solace of words; their sound, their rhythm gave him comfort, restored him, as it were, to himself. It was natural enough. It was indeed laudable. After an irreparable loss the human being must survive, ought to survive by whatever means are available. For Raymond writing was the immediate refuge. We hoped it would be a lasting one. For he enjoyed writing. He said so; and clearly he found in it none of the pain which for many writers accompanies the pleasure. How else to explain a letter to Leonard about football and the rewards of 'amateur' sport? The occasion was the rejection by the *Sunday Times* of one of his stories; but the greater part of the text was an analysis of American football, 'the finest game in the world as a spectacle'. He examined the role of the coach. Then: 'Over here when a promising high school football player is approached by an unofficial representative of a university to register there and come out for football, as we say, he doesn't bother asking about what sort of an education he is going to get, he just asks how much money he is going to be paid.' The letter, in single-space typing, ran on for three packed pages. At the end, a postscript in his own hand. 'How the hell did I ever get started on that subject?'

When we saw him again he did not at first seem greatly altered. He came back to England in the spring of 1955; we gave dinner-parties for him. Once we asked Ian Fleming to meet him; Raymond brought Jessica Tyndale, a composed and agreeable American who had befriended him on the voyage over; Ronald Howe, at the time Deputy Commissioner at New Scotland Yard and a mine of criminal intelligence, was in the party. Raymond was in relaxed form; I think that was the time when, as late at night we gathered in the hall to collect coats and scarves, he flung his arms round my neck and exclaimed loudly: 'When do we get down to the serious necking?' We were always happy in our meetings with him. But gradually we recognized a change. We heard from friends of days when he had accepted an invitation – and failed to appear. Reported misadventures of this sort made one nervous about arranging a dinner. One was thankful for an assurance that he would turn up, and I remember once responding with something like effusiveness to his question, an hour or so beforehand, might he bring a girl with him? She was, perhaps, poor girl, a trifle daunted by the company in which she found herself, and one of our more literary women guests viewed her with disapproval. Still, the evening went off without mishap.

Presently Raymond – Ray, by that time, in his letters – returned to America. When he came back here we felt that he was drifting in more senses than one. I was among several friends to whom he sent short stories, tiny sketches of sexual encounters which at the time seemed dimly pornographic. I had a little packet of them, long since lost. Today one would think them the most innocuous of fantasies. They had no talent that I could discern; impossible to express any judgment on them, and I fancy that after a while I stopped acknowledging them. I was obscurely aware that Raymond was in need of some sort of help. Perhaps I should have tried. But I knew I was not equipped to offer it, and presently I heard that other people, worthier, more compassionate, perhaps with more time on their hands, had gone to his rescue. Leonard and I were not the friends he needed.

Looking back now, I realize that, leaving aside the brilliant literary gifts which first seduced me, I like Raymond best in his relationship with Cissy, that smiling, propitiatory figure whom he guarded and defended. And created: she lives on in his image of her, the adored creature to be consulted, encouraged, constantly and proudly displayed. Marlowe was his fantasy image of himself, tough and daring in a world without Cissy. In a world with Cissy he showed another kind of gallantry; he shielded her. And he needed her. Without her he had lost not only his accustomed place in the everyday world but the entry to his own world of fable; the decay of his working years after her death is proof of that. Whatever his errancies, she was the stable point in the life of reality.

We met him many more times than we met her. But I can no longer summon up his image. It is Cissy whom I see: the fading eyes in the drained face, the look – I know now what it was – of appeal.

Marlowe,
Men And Women

MICHAEL MASON

In the closing chapter of *Love And Death In The American Novel* Leslie Fiedler has this to say about the modern American thriller:

Murder laced with lust, mayhem spiced with nymphomania: this is the formula for the chief surviving form of the murder mystery in America, though, indeed, that form has not surrendered its native birthright of anti-feminism. It insists, however, on undressing its bitches, surveying them with a surly and concupiscent eye before punching, shooting, or consigning them to the gas-chamber. Not only in the cruder and more successful books of Mickey Spillane, but in the more pretentious ones of Raymond Chandler, the detective story has reverted to the kind of populist semi-pornography that once made George Lippard's *The Monks of Monk Hall* a black-market bestseller.

It is striking to find in this clever and subversive book a judgment that seems to spring more from an inaccurate stereotype about Chandler than from his text – especially as the whole thrust of Fiedler's account of American fiction is to stress certain sexual themes of which Chandler's novels could very readily have provided further illustration. If Professor Fiedler can so misrepresent Chandler's fiction it is no surprise that the generality of his readers, has failed to discern what is characteristic in his treatment of sexuality. The stereotype is clearly wrong: in no sense do Chandler's novels consist of 'populist semi-pornography' and 'mayhem spiced with nymphomania'. Fiedler does concede that the type of thriller in question 'has not surrendered its native birthright of anti-feminism', but for Chandler's fiction this way of putting the matter is too unemphatic, and anti-feminism in Chandler is anyway only one of a cluster of themes that give the novels a strongly homosexual cast.

James Cain's *Double Indemnity* of 1945 is a short thriller that fits Fiedler's description somewhat better, and in Chandler's reworking of it for the cinema it is possible actually to see him putting distance between himself and his more orthodox model in the handling of sexuality. The Keyes–Walter bond (in the film: Edward G. Robinson and Fred MacMurray) which is the emotional core of Chandler's script is wholly absent from Cain's novel; Keyes is just a dislikeable threat to Walter's plans: 'big and fat and peevish'. Of course the comradeship of Keyes and Walter in Chandler's version is only homosexual in tone, not in fact. Indeed if Chandler, while working on *Double Indemnity*, still felt about Cain's fiction the way he had a few months earlier, he probably thought of the comradeship theme as a sexually cleansing element:

> But James Cain – faugh! Everything he touches smells like a billygoat. He is every kind of writer I detest, a *faux naïf*, a Proust in greasy overalls, a dirty little boy with a piece of chalk and a board fence and nobody looking. Such people are the offal of literature, not because they write about dirty things, but because they do it in a dirty way. Nothing hard and clean and cold and ventilated. A brothel with a smell of cheap scent in the front parlour and a bucket of slops at the back door.

This extraordinarily shrill passage in a letter to Alfred Knopf in 1943 is almost embarrassing in its betrayal of revulsion from heterosexuality ('billygoat ... offal ... brothel ... cheap scent ... slops'). Chandler may have thought of his picture of male comradeship in *Double Indemnity* as healthily unsexual, but it is in truth more like a plea for another kind of sexuality, alternative to the heterosexual bond.

Admittedly the stress on masculine comradeship is the one respect in which Chandler's minor fiction – that is, the short stories and film-scripts – is noticeably idiosyncratic about sex; this theme is particularly insistent in the scripts. The other tokens of a homosexual interest in Chandler's fiction – misogyny, a relish for certain male characters, and femininity in the hero – are almost entirely confined to the novels. So something of a case could be made for the view that these features are byproducts of a special formal undertaking: the extended narrative of crime and detection which is part of a sequence of similar narratives about the same hero. For example, Chandler himself suggested in 'The Simple Art of Murder' that 'the whole point is that the detective exists complete and entire and unchanged by anything that happens ... That is why he never gets the girl, never marries' (one difficulty for this as a rule about Chandler's hero is of course that Chandler experimented – infelicitously, it is true – with a married Marlowe in his unfinished novel, *The Poodle Springs Mystery*). Again, the extraordinary regularity with which the villains of these novels turn out to be women may be explicable simply on the grounds of mystery: the longer the whodunit the more unguessable the solution has to be, and the reader is fairly unlikely to entertain the idea of a female murderer. The oddity of the notion may be its very point. Certainly it does happen that where Chandler has developed a novel out of an earlier short story what is offered as a provisional and too obvious solution in the novel was the authentic, final solution in the shorter version (compare the story of 'The Lady in the Lake', published in *Dime Detective Magazine* in 1939, with the novel of the same title; in the former the Derace Kingsley character *does* kill the Crystal Kingsley character).

Perhaps there are further aspects of sexuality in the Marlowe books which can be referred in some way to functional considerations like these. But my guess is that there would remain a great excess of un-explained material and feeling – homosexual in import – however thoroughly the functional argument were pressed. I think that homosex-ual motifs are more conspicuous in the novels than in the stories and filmscripts simply because Chandler took the former more seriously, and this included putting more of his personal concerns into them. The novel he took most seriously of all, *The Long Goodbye*, is more em-phatically, even overtly, a novel of homosexual feeling than any of the others.

Chandler's formula about Marlowe's success with women is, after all, misleading. The statement that Marlowe 'never gets the girl' asserts something not strictly true, and implies something generally false, to wit, that not 'getting the girl' is a misfortune for Marlowe. To leave aside for the moment his uncharacteristic display of sexual avidity in *Play-back*, Marlowe does at the end of *The Long Goodbye* 'get the girl' in the fullest sense in the shape of Linda Loring. But the episode is extra-ordinarily devoid of eroticism. There is not the faintest allusion to Mar-lowe's actually feeling desire for Linda. The only affective physical detail about her is one 'long dark hair' she leaves on Marlowe's pillow, and this least vital component of a human body, bloodless and nerveless – and in this case separated from the body anyway – is used by Chandler not to promote desire in Marlowe but rather the chill consciousness of Linda's absence.

Warm, erotic feeling and loving contact with a woman are irreconcil-able for Marlowe. He falls more swiftly and completely in love with Mrs Eddie Mars (in *The Big Sleep*) than with any other woman, but her physi-cal appearance – also specified by her hair – is weirdly inorganic: 'She was so platinumed that her hair shone like a fruit bowl.' Again, the hair is not even attached to her body:

'It's a wig, silly ...' She reached up and yanked it off. Her own hair was clipped short all over, like a boy's.

(Incidentally when this character first appears, in the short story 'The Curtain' – *Black Mask*, 1936 – she wears 'a green travelling dress with a mannish cut to it'). Marlowe's brief physical contact with Mrs Mars is suitably, if extravagantly, unsensual:

> Her face under my mouth was like ice. She put her hands up and took hold of my head and kissed me hard on the lips. Her lips were like ice, too.
> I went out through the door and it closed behind me without sound, and the rain blew in under the porch, not as cold as her lips.

These two paragraphs deliver with striking literalness the qualities Chandler missed in Cain's writing: something 'hard and clean and cold and ventilated'.

Marlowe found Linda Loring's 'long dark hair' the next morning when he 'pulled the bed to pieces and remade it'. Apart from illustrating Marlowe's unmasculine assiduity in domestic chores this action may remind the reader of an episode in another novel which has a very different narrative context, but perhaps not such a different feeling; after all, a bed does not have to be completely unmade before it can be made, and certainly not 'pulled ... to pieces'. When Marlowe in *The Big Sleep* has ejected Carmen Sternwood from his bed, into which she has climbed uninvited, Chandler resorts to a strikingly similar expression: 'I ... tore the bed to pieces savagely'. And in this different context, of disgust for a woman, the tokens of physicality (so meagre when Chandler is trying to indicate an affirmative heterosexual impulse) are abundantly deployed: Carmen's 'blonde head', 'bare arms', 'slaty eyes', 'small sharp teeth', 'round and naughty eyes', and finally her body 'naked and glistening' are all specified. The loathed Carmen does not leave behind on the bed just a long dark hair, but the whole 'imprint of her head ... of her small corrupt body'. Although Chandler's biographer, Frank Mac-Shane, likes to attribute heterosexual practices to both Chandler and his hero even when this entails tampering with the evidence, he has to concede that Marlowe's destruction of the bed in *The Big Sleep* 'is an extraordinarily violent reaction'.

When Marlowe does become properly aroused by a woman the narrative has a macabre way of showing how reprehensible this is. The most brutal murders in the Marlowe novels are committed by women with whom the hero has had an erotically exciting contact. Mrs Grayle, in

Farewell, My Lovely, falls across Marlowe's lap and he begins to 'browse' on her face:

> She worked her eyelashes and made butterfly kisses on my cheeks. When I got to her mouth it was half open and burning and her tongue was a darting snake between her teeth.

This is the woman who pounds Linsday Marriott's head until he has 'brains on his face':

> His hair was dark with blood, the beautiful blond ledges were tangled with blood, and some thick greyish ooze, like primeval slime.

Eileen Wade also employs a darting tongue, and other stimuli as well:

> She pressed herself hard against me and her hair brushed my face. Her mouth came up to be kissed. She was trembling. Her lips opened and her teeth opened and her tongue darted. Then her hands dropped and jerked at something and the robe she was wearing came open, and underneath it she was as naked as September Morn but a darn sight less coy.
>
> 'Put me on the bed,' she breathed.
>
> I did that. Putting my arms around her I touched bare skin, soft skin, soft, yielding flesh. I lifted her and carried her the few steps to the bed and lowered her. She kept her arms around my neck. She was making some kind of a whistling noise in her throat. Then she threshed about and moaned. This was murder. I was erotic as a stallion.

Murder indeed. Eileen Wade has recently beaten Sylia Lennox's head into a 'bloody sponge' (the Lennox butler, according to the investigating sergeant, 'don't recognize her by her face. She practically ain't got one'). There is actually a serious point to be made concerning Marlowe's unfortunate phrase about his reaction to Eileen Wade's overtures: this expression and the following one ('I was erotic as a stallion') have a derisive jauntiness to them that quite disrupts the otherwise fairly convincing, if cliché-dependent, mood of heterosexual arousal. A similar note is struck by Marlowe's 'browsing' on Mrs Grayle's face (an image, like that of the stallion, which betrays Chandler's conviction of the animality of such proceedings).

These cases show very well how the evil of Chandler's villainesses goes well beyond anything required by their function as keys to a whodunit. Chandler casts women in this role so regularly that an attentive reader of the Marlowe novels will soon find his guess about the identity of the villain easy to make, so the device is not even a very good one for securing mystification. In four out of the seven completed novels the chief culprit is a woman: *The Big Sleep* (Carmen Sternwood), *Farewell, My Lovely* (Mrs Grayle), *The Lady in the Lake* (Muriel Chess), and *The Long Goodbye* (Eileen Wade). In the more complex solutions of *The High Window* and *The Little Sister* an important proportion of the murders is done by women: Mrs Murdock, Orfamy Quest and Dolores Gonzales. So the only Chandler novel in which nobody is murdered by a woman is *Playback*.

The general effect is that Chandler's world is morally skewed in a way that makes nonsense of the author's claim, which he liked to imply if not actually state, that the Marlowe novels are edifyingly clear-sighted about good and evil. Their moral scheme is in truth pathologically harsh on women, and pathologically lenient towards men. For just as the novels are full of homicidal females – gunning men down, beating their brains out, and pushing them out of windows – they are correspondingly devoid of bad males. There is scarcely a dislikeable man to be found, and even the initially dislikeable, especially among the police, often turn out to be less unpleasant than they seemed.

But nothing betrays Chandler's bias more damagingly here than the treatment of male criminals – not the agents of the acts of homicide on which the narratives turn, but the agents of the mass crime that is so sententiously depicted in *The Long Goodbye*:

> Twenty-four hours a day somebody is running, somebody else is trying to catch him. Out there in the night of a thousand crimes people were dying, being maimed, cut by flying glass, crushed against steering wheels or under heavy tires. People were being beaten, robbed, strangled, raped, and murdered.

The most notable representative of the lower levels of professional crime in the Marlowe novels is Moose Malloy. Before we are ten pages into *Farewell, My Lovely* this violent, oafish simpleton has gratuitously broken a man's neck; soon afterwards he strangles Mrs Florian and knocks her brains out on the bedpost. But Marlowe continues to feel for him a mixture of tenderness and boyish admiration. What could be more morally obtuse? Perhaps only the indulgence extended by

Chandler to the higher echelons of organized crime. The more comprehensive a man's responsibility for the 'night of a thousand crimes', the more engaging and kindly he is likely to be in a Marlowe novel. In *The Big Sleep* the reader does not meet the ex-bootlegger Rusty Regan, whose magnetic charm gives the plot its initial impetus, but General Sternwood paints his picture: 'a big curly-haired Irishman from Clonmel, with sad eyes and a smile as wide as Wilshire Boulevard'. We do meet Eddie Mars, a 'top-flight racketeer' in Los Angeles: he is always polite, he has 'a nice easy smile' and 'thoughtful grey eyes', 'he looked hard, not the hardness of the tough guy. More like the hardness of a well-weathered horseman'. (Something 'hard and ventilated' again – on top of the Los Angeles dunghill.) Laird Brunette of *Farewell, My Lovely* is at least as powerful as Eddie Mars and he is just as gentle, healthy-looking and polite. Alex Morny of *The High Window* is smaller fry – only a night-club and casino owner with 'plenty of protection' – but he has a disarmingly 'handsome face' and eyebrows with 'an elegant curve'. Steelgrave in *The Little Sister* (alias Weepy Moyer, a highgrade professional killer from Chicago) matches Mars and Brunette in gentleness and civility. In *The Long Goodbye* Marlowe only speaks to Randy Starr – Las Vagas racketeer – on the telephone, but Starr talks 'mildly and quietly', in a 'quiet, competent, man-of-affairs voice'.

The American writer Gershon Legman seems to have been the first critic to notice Marlowe's susceptibility to male charm, and he drew the obvious conclusion. His hint came from the very blatant description of Red Norgaard ('probably the nicest man I ever met') in *Farewell, My Lovely*:

> He had the eyes you never see, that you only read about. Violet eyes. Almost purple. Eyes like a girl, a lovely girl. His skin was as soft as silk. Lightly reddened, but it would never tan. It was too delicate ... He was not as big as Moose Malloy, but he looked very fast on his feet.

Norgaard may not be as big as Moose Malloy, but he shares with him the appeal that so bewitches Marlowe's moral sense where the latter is concerned:

> His voice was soft, dreamy, so delicate for a big man that it was startling. It made me think of another soft-voiced big man I had strangely liked.

MARLOWE, MEN AND WOMEN

That word 'strangely' is pounced on by Legman in his book, *Love and Death: A Study in Censorship*:

> No matter how 'strangely' Chandler's detective, Marlowe, moons over these big men, they are always beating him up ... The true explanation of Marlowe's temperamental disinterest in women is not 'honour', but his interest in men ... Chandler's Marlowe is clearly homosexual – a butterfly, as the Chinese say, dreaming that he is a man.

Legman has noticed another respect in which the vaunted moral scheme of the Marlowe novels is vitiated by homosexual bias. Interestingly enough, the book in which Marlowe's honour is most clearly a disguise for homosexual feeling. *The Long Goodbye*, was yet to be published when Legman wrote these words.

Moose Malloy does not really 'beat up' Marlowe, but the suggestion that Marlowe likes to be attacked and physically defeated by strong men is interesting. Marlowe's backchat is famous, but he deploys it with strange consistency to taunt males who have him physically in their power. Partly it is the sheer volubility which irritates them, a volubility they find uncomfortably out of place in this husky, virile-looking man. Of course the tension between Marlowe's looks and his personality is in general a deliberate thing on Chandler's part, and one important function it performs is to stress Marlowe's unusual intelligence. But part of the slight shock the reader feels when the owner of the clever, chattering narrative voice is suddenly seen from the outside (as when Mrs Regan calls him a 'big dark handsome brute') may be the sense of something sexually anamolous in the contrast.

Chandler had earlier developed this aspect of the narrative voice in an extraordinary way in the short story 'Pearls Are a Nuisance' (*Dime Detective Magazine*, 1939) – a work exceptional among the minor fiction for its degree of bizarre sexual feeling. The whole interest of the character of the hero, Walter, is the piquant, indeed fantastic contrast between his tough, hard-drinking exterior and the ornate British English idiom in which he thinks and talks. Walter forms a sudden, close bond with an even tougher, more hard-drinking crook called Henry Eichelberger, and while the two are working on the crime together they have to avoid Walter's fiancée, Ellen. The arrangement becomes strongly suggestive of competing sexual loyalties, especially at such moments as the two men's awakening on the same bed after a heavy drinking session ('Henry Eichelberger was lying beside me in his undershirt and trousers.).

Clearly this is the topic – the femininity of Marlowe's nature – about which it is most difficult to produce hard evidence. People have differing views on what constitutes femininity in a personality, and anyway the argument depends on Chandler's opinions on the matter, which are an unknown quantity. But I would adduce also Marlowe's domesticity, which I mentioned earlier: not only the frequent bed-making, but the airing of rooms (the ventilation obsession again), emptying of ashtrays and careful brewing of coffee (Marlowe must be among the very few detectives in fiction to give a policeman a recipe for making coffee, which he does in *Farewell, My Lovely*). Although there is an attempt by Chandler to represent Marlowe's domestic base as minimal and characterless ('a place to keep his clothes' as Chandler called it in 'The Simple Art of Murder') there is in the novels a distinct competing strand of attention to this environment; the reader gets some idea of its character in most of the Marlowe books. The greatest weight of domestic detail is reserved for the house on Yucca Avenue in *The Long Goodbye*. We learn about the awkward front steps, the overgrown garden, the automatic timer in the kitchen, the trapdoor to the loft, the mail-box with the damaged woodpecker on top, the garbage can under the sink, the venetian blinds. We also witness Marlowe at his most houseproud, serving coffee for Eileen Wade:

> I went out to the kitchen and spread a paper napkin on a green metal tray. It looked as cheesy as a celluloid collar. I crumpled it up and got out one of those fringed things that come in sets with little triangular napkins. They came with the house, like most of the furniture. I set out two Desert Rose coffee cups and filled them and carried the tray in.

Or perhaps 'house-humble' is the appropriate term; it is not the domestic knick-knacks that Marlowe dislikes here, but their inelegance (they denote a lack of womanly activity just as a 'celluloid collar' does).

Chandler probably read Gershon Legman's remarks about Marlowe in 1951, when *The Long Goodbye* was still at an early stage of composition. They did not deter him from carrying on and completing a novel that is susceptible of a homosexual reading in ways too obvious to need mention, and which actually contains a conversation between Roger Wade and Marlowe about homosexuality in fiction. On the other hand the letter which Chandler wrote about Legman certainly suggests that he applied the latter's remarks to the novel he was then working on. Legman had noticed Marlowe's dislike of women and his physical relish for men, but Chandler speaks as if the nub of the matter were the idea of male comradeship, a topic not mentioned by Legman but central, of course, to *The Long Goodbye*:

> Mr Legman seems to me to belong to that rather numerous class of American neurotics which cannot conceive of a close friendship between a couple of men as other than homosexual.

The rather one-sided conversation between Wade and Marlowe also sounds like an oblique retort by Chandler to the charge that his novels are homosexual in feeling. Or so it appears at first – for the curious feature of the episode is how Wade's wool-gathering about homosexuality amounts to a defence, not of the heterosexual probity of his fiction, but of the naturalness of a homosexual element in literature. It concludes with one of those passages of vehement disgust about female sexuality so characteristic of Chandler.

'I had a male secretary once. Used to dictate to him. Let him go. He bothered me sitting there waiting for me to create. Mistake. Ought to have kept him. Word would have got around I was a homo. The clever boys that write book reviews because they can't write anything else would have caught on and started giving me the build-up. Have to take care of their own, you know. They're all queers, every damn one of them. The queer is the artistic arbiter of our age, chum. The pervert is the top guy now.'

'That so? Always been around, hasn't he?'

He wasn't looking at me. He was just talking. But he heard what I said.

'Sure, thousands of years. And especially in all the great ages of art. Athens, Rome, the Renaissance, the Elizabethan Age, the Romantic Movement in France – loaded with them. Queers all over the place. Ever read *The Golden Bough*? No, too long for you. Shorter version though. Ought to read it. Proves our sexual habits are pure convention – like wearing a black tie with a dinner jacket. Me, I'm a sex writer, but with frills and straight.'

He looked up at me and sneered. 'You know something? I'm a liar. My heroes are eight feet tall and my heroines have callouses on their bottoms from lying in bed with their knees up. Lace and ruffles, swords and coaches, elegance and leisure, duels and gallant death. All lies. They used perfume instead of soap, their teeth rotted because they never cleaned them, their fingernails smelled of stale gravy. The nobility of France urinated against the walls in the marble corridors of Versailles, and when you finally got several sets of underclothes off the lovely marquise the first thing you noticed was that she needed a bath. I ought to write it that way.'

Roger Wade could take a broad view of the homosexual's role in European culture, but his creator did not feel able to venture down this path beyond the point he had reached with *The Long Goodbye*. Indeed there are clear signs of a frightened recoil. Chandler's next novel and his last complete one, *Playback*, exhibits an extraordinary reversal of some of the most consistent tokens of Marlowe's sexual nature. The plot exactly inverts that of *The Long Goodbye*, since it turns on Marlowe's irrational loyalty to a woman, Berry Mayfield, who like Terry Lennox is suspected of a crime. He makes love to her several times; she even has orgasms. There is a brave attempt to make Marlowe behave like a sadistic, rampant thriller-hero:

> She started for the door, but I caught her by the wrist and spun her around. The torn blouse didn't reveal any startling nakedness, merely some skin and part of a brassiere. You'd see more on the beach, far more, but you wouldn't see it through a torn blouse.
> I must have been leering a little because she suddenly curled her fingers and tried to claw me.
> 'I'm no bitch in heat,' she said between tight teeth. 'Take your paws off me.'
> I got the other wrist and started to pull her closer. She tried to knee me in the groin, but she was already too close. Then she went limp and pulled her head back and closed her eyes.

Interestingly this is also the one book in which Marlowe does not have a domestic base. The investigation, and the sex, is peripatetic, and for most of the novel Marlowe is staying in a motel.

Playback has always been the black sheep among Chandler's novels for his readers, a forgettable work that somehow does not belong in the canon, which suggests how necessary the homosexual side of Marlowe was for Chandler's peculiar kind of excellence. The piece of sadistic sexuality from *Playback* quoted above is the only passage in Chandler's novels which even approximates to the Fiedler stereotype of 'mayhem spiced with nymphomania'. Yet this is still seen as the typical mode of the Marlowe novels by a critic as intelligent as Fiedler – and despite Gershon Legman's much earlier remarks on the subject. In 1974 a film-maker, Robert Altman, expressed a deeper understanding of Marlowe's nature than most of the literary critics. The Marlowe in his version of of *The Long Goodbye* is accused of being a 'faggot', is seen to be un-interested in the most voluptuous women, and talks to himself in a soft jabber that nicely corresponds to the unmasculine voice of Chandler's narrative. But Altman does not allow Marlowe's dream of love for Terry Lennox to remain as untarnished as it does in Chandler's novel. In this film Lennox is a murderer and a cheat. The closing shot is a careful imitation of the closing shot in *The Third Man*, a brilliant cinematic allusion to indicate that Terry Lennox's depravity is like that of Harry Lime, and Marlowe's disillusion as profound as that of the sexually ambiguous Holly Martins.

Autumn In London

MICHAEL GILBERT

I met the works of Raymond Chandler ten years before I met their author.

It was the last Christmas of World War II. We were out of the line, enjoying a well-timed rest in a village on the Adriatic coast of Italy so small that I have never been able to rediscover it on any map. Our billet was an old Italian villa which had clearly been laid out with an eye to coolness during the long Italian summer. This was the Italian winter, and it was very cold indeed. There was not a lot to do in the evenings except sit round an oil-drip stove, which had been constructed by the Divisional Sappers and was so effective that it ultimately blew up and burned down the villa. It was in these propitious circumstances that I first encountered *The Lady in the Lake.*

A kind friend had sent it out from England. She had written on the fly leaf: 'I'm told that Raymond Chandler is just one of Peter Cheyney's many pen-names.' When I had read ten pages I took out my own pen and wrote underneath: 'If Raymond Chandler is Peter Cheyney, I am the Archbishop of Canterbury.' I still have the book with this early piece of literary analysis in it.

(In my view *The Lady in the Lake* is, by a short head, the finest of Chandler's books. There is no physical violence in the first hundred pages of any sort, yet the whole thing crackles with that inimitable Chandler electricity; every sentence a tiny spark, every paragraph craftily put together by a literary electronics engineer.)

In the decade after the war, I read and enjoyed the other three which make up that great quartet of books, *Farewell, My Lovely, The High Window* and *The Big Sleep* – never quite matched, alas, in any subsequent works. If they had been allowed to stand by themselves they would have formed as astonishing a corpus of work as the four novels of Dashiell Hammett; who was, incidentally, the only contemporary writer to whom Chandler ever made obeisance.

It had never occurred to me that I might have a chance of meeting the author, whom I had pictured as safely tucked away on the West Coast of America in whatever seaside resort corresponded to his fictional Bay City; keeping, I hoped, on better terms with the local police than Marlowe did. I was therefore delighted when I heard, early in 1955 from Dorothy Gardiner, who was at that time secretary of the Mystery Writers of America (a body in close correspondence with our own newly formed Crime Writers Association) that Chandler was not only coming over to England but had expressed a wish to meet me. Would I like to? Would I, hell!

I am far from sure what sort of person I expected to meet. I repeated to myself the advice given to the young lady by Conan Doyle when she accused him of being Sherlock Holmes – 'Pray get this into your cerebral tentacle: the doll and its maker are seldom identical.' Nonetheless, subconsciously I must have been looking for someone in the Marlowe mould. It was with something of a shock, therefore, that the mild, friendly-looking man with the brushed-back grey hair and glasses was pointed out to me as Raymond Chandler.

The mildness – as I was to discover – was temporary. Ray, as I shall call him from now on, since he immediately asked me to do so, was *not* normally a mild man. He was capable of being more abrasive with tongue and pen than almost anyone I have known. The impression of friendliness, on the other hand, was correct.

It has to be borne in mind – and everything which I say from now on has to be qualified by the fact – that I am talking about the last years of Ray's life. Those who have read the various accounts of that life will know that he had recently lost his wife, Cissy, who had been the mainstay and sheet anchor of his existence. It was the autumn period. The mists which enveloped him five years later had begun to drift up. But nothing could obscure his fundamental likeability. With the possible exception of Customs Officers and Tax Inspectors he was prepared to be friends with everyone he met. It was a friendship which was far from superficial. To be taken into it was like coming out of the cold into a warm and well-lit room.

I have little recollection of what we talked about on that first evening at the Connaught Hotel. We probably discussed fellow crime-writers in England and America. He expressed admiration for Ian Fleming, and thought the torture scene in *Casino Royale* the most effective thing of its sort he had ever read. 'Cultured brutality' was the expression he used. What was clear to me was that Ray was going to be a great success in England and I left the hotel with regret that I should probably never have a legitimate excuse for meeting such an attractive person again. His letter arrived a few weeks later. It was, like all his letters, on light blue paper, in dark blue type – a colour combination which achieved the pleasing effect of an old Etonian tie. It was the first of nearly a hundred which were to arrive over the next five years. Small blue bombshells among my humdrum mail. It started 'Dear Gilbert'. By the time the second letter arrived this uncharacteristic formality had, I am glad to say, been dropped in favour of 'Dear Mike'.

It said: 'If you are in a proper kind of law practice I should very much like to consult you professionally about the problems of my living in England without being disastrously shattered by taxes and so forth.' This was the root problem and was to recur: but there were others as well. There was the vexed question of his residence permit. This gave rise to a series of brushes between Ray and officialdom:

> The last sordid episode in my struggle to comply with the Alien Registration Law was enacted today. Yesterday, in spite of repeated assurances that I need not register, I received a stern letter from the Commissioner of Police (by remote control) demanding that I present myself at the earliest possible moment with two passport photographs, my travel documents and 5/–. This I did this morning, only to be greeted as a VIP, ushered into a private office and smiled upon. An entry was made in the Day Book (a dog-eared ledger which appeared to have been lying in an attic for a couple of hundred years), my passport was stamped and my passport photographs and the five shillings were waved away as not worth consideration. I asked: 'Are you quite sure, gentlemen' – for there were two of them, both very gentlemanly – 'that I shall not be receiving any more stern notes from the Commissioner of Police?' They were quite sure, but the way this thing has been handled, I wouldn't believe anything anyone (including yourself) said. I am out 15 bob for the passport photos and at least thirty bob for various taxis to get this done. I AM NOT AMUSED. Or am I? Of course, the passport photos do redeem it somewhat. There never was a more perfectly cast dope-smuggler. If I could play the piano I might qualify for a role as an ace-operative in the Abwehr. The type that plays Scarlatti whilst toe nails are being pulled out.

The photographs continued to fascinate Ray, who eventually sent me one. He had abandoned the idea of it being a dope smuggler and now thought that it made him look like a bulldog with stomach-ache. (In a later letter Ray mentioned that Dorothy Gardiner had been caught up with by the authorities in Oakham when *she* first came to England. The police then discovered that they hadn't actually got an Aliens Register. 'Think of it, Mike! The first alien in Rutlandshire.')

The time-table of Ray's first visit – and, indeed, of all his visits – was dominated by the looming presence of the Tax Inspector. The general rule, which he understood, was that if he stayed in England for more than six months in any fiscal year he would have to pay English tax on money which he earned in, or brought into, England. This did not stop him, on the first occasion, from staying for much longer than six months. His view of tax inspectors was that they could be dodged if you were quick enough on your feet, or fooled if you were smart enough. He booked his flight back to America for 6 October. For the moment this was safe enough. Although his overall stay was very nearly six months, he had been away to Italy for a fortnight in the middle of it. I had lunch with him at the Garrick two days before he left. When I said I imagined that the next time I would see him would be after 5 April 1956 he agreed that this would be prudent. Had I known him better I would have taken this with a large pinch of Garrick salt. The next letter to arrive was a handwritten scrawl, less than six weeks later. 'I'm back again! Had a little trouble getting past immigration. Six months almost up. I suppose I shall be stuck for some British tax.'

The next thing I heard, through his doctor, was the unhappy news that Ray had been taken ill, and admitted to the London Clinic in a coma. He seems to have been in and out of nursing homes for about a month. A letter dated 2 February, evidently in answer to one of mine, starts: 'I'm not well yet, but I'm improving. Tax is still my main preoccupation. A friend of mine happens to be one of a banking family. It appears from what I'm told (by their tax experts) that if I do not sign a lease or acquire property and the record shows my visits to England to be sporadic, then it is unlikely they would bother me.' As it happened, either the experts had misinformed Ray, or he had misquoted the experts. More of that anon. On 11 May he wrote to say goodbye for the time being. 'I think your most urgent job for me, apart from making me a will, is to find out in a discrete way when I can come back again.'

This was the heart of the matter. It is quite clear that Ray yearned to come back to London. There were people there whom he liked being with, and who liked being with him. Also, he found that he was a bigger literary lion in England than he had been in America and he never made any secret of the fact that he enjoyed being lionized. The guardian who stood with drawn sword barring the gate of this particular Eden was the taxman. In his first and longest visit Ray considerably outstayed his six-month allowance for 1955/6. He had arrived on 19 April and did not finally leave until 11 May in the following year. Even allowing for his abortive scuttle back to the States in October and for two short trips abroad, one to Italy and one to Morocco, he had overdrawn his account by nearly ninety days ('No way round it, I'm afraid, Mike. The dates are all in my passport').

The precise details of a man's tax difficulties interest only himself and the inspector. In any event even a summary of the dozens of letters which passed between us on this topic would make tedious reading. Ray, as he was fond of mentioning, had spent a longer period of his life as a businessman than he had as a writer, and his letters were packed with unanswerable questions. Was the money which he brought over taxable here as income if he could show that it had been capital when it left America? Was he a visitor, an immigrant, or a returning British citizen? (Not an easy question, as will be seen.) Was he working as an author in England if he didn't actually write anything? Surely an author was working when he was thinking out his plots? I did my best, but I cannot feel that it was an entirely satisfactory best. Ray was tolerant of my efforts, but concluded that he would have to get a more expert opinion:

Your letter of 29 March reached me yesterday. It is full of beautiful words. But it seems somehow to evade the issues that really worry me. These answers are vital to me, because I have various reasons for wanting to return to London. Because I want to see if I can write a play; because I have some very dear friends there; because the atmosphere is congenial to me – although the climate is not.

Even with the help of tax accountants and tax counsel some of these conundrums were never really answered. By the end I am not even sure that Ray really expected an answer:

I understand how difficult it is to deal with these people. My then American tax lawyer couldn't make head or tail of the Taxes Act which you sent to me and I sent on to him. He said it was such a jumbled lot of nonsense that he wouldn't even read it through. I gather that with you practice and case law and so forth mean more than anything else. Here the Law, although sometimes debatable, is at least intelligible. With you it seems to be mostly a matter of negotiation.

One of the facts which one might have imagined to be crystal clear was the question of Ray's nationality. His father was American, he had been born in in America, had married an American woman, and had lived and worked in America for most of his life. However, things were not as simple as they seemed; with Ray, they seldom were. Ray's mother, British born, had divorced his father when Ray was very young, returned with him to England, and resumed her British nationality. This led to a fine tangle which Ray finally, as he thought, disentangled by instituting an action against the American Attorney General in Los Angeles. This was long before I knew him – in 1948. The judgment of the Southern District Court of California seemed quite clear: 'Plaintiff at all times since his birth and up to and including the date of the filing of the Complaint herein has been a citizen of the United States. The [previous] rulings of the United States Department of Justice and Immigration and Naturalization Service to the effect that the Plaintiff was not a citizen of the United States were and are erroneous.'

However. 30 March:

Yesterday I received a body-blow from the British Consulate. I told you I had filed an application to be admitted to England as a resident. They sent this on to the Home Office, who replied that it could not be granted since the British Government still regarded me as a British National *in spite of the decision of the Federal Court.* If I applied for a British passport it would be given me, but then our Government would rule that by making this application I was voluntarily expatriating myself, and would refuse me an American passport.

This was the sort of snarl Ray always seemed to be getting himself into. He pictured himself, I am sure, as Laocoon entwined by the serpents of officialdom, struggling desperately to free an arm or a leg, only to become more and more irrevocably gripped and throttled. I think he actually enjoyed piling on the agony. 'And this would only be the beginning. When I came back to America I should only be allowed to enter as a visitor or as an immigrant – into my own country! And when I entered England as a British national, I should become subject to all the currency restrictions and might be forced to convert my American assets into sterling.'

These paper battles would not have mattered so much if they had not had the effect of keeping in America a very human and likeable person who was longing to be in England. 'The whole trouble with this damned nonsense is that although tax laws may be drawn up by experts they are enacted by politicians. For the life of me I cannot understand why a country which needs dollars should penalize people for bringing dollars into it. I suppose the answer is that in this age men are ruled by pressures and not by principles.'

So it was to be nearly two years before we saw Ray again. He wrote from Palm Springs early in 1957; 'On Monday I return to La Jolla, rather lonely and rather sad. I have a book to finish and a life, for which I have no great regard, to live.' But it must not be supposed that Ray was always gloomy. Cheerfulness kept breaking in. It was in the same letter that he recorded, in a purple passage, his ideas on taking a lady out to dinner:

The technique is absolute, although rather demeaning. You make a booking in advance and say what sort of table you want. You arrive, and your car is taken away by an attendant in uniform. You enter, and are greeted by the maître d'hotel (they have half a dozen captains) and you say: 'Good evening, I believe I had a reservation but possibly you could not manage to give me the table I rather wanted.' At the same time you slip a folded five dollar bill into his hand. Now, in this part of the country very few people do that. They demand, they do not politely ask, and above all they do not themselves provide the maître d'hotel, in advance, with a situation for which he may only have to offer the mildest apology. As a result of this approach (and the five bucks) you get the best table in the house, and the captains won't even let the waiters wait on you, or pour the wine. You can't light your own cigarette. The lighter is already there as you put it to your mouth. It amazes me how few Americans understand the art of combining generosity in tipping with demanding very little. But that is the whole point. These headwaiters are tough, callous and cynical, but they must behave with deference to the most impossible people. Then someone comes along who treats *them* with deference, and they simply can't do enough for you. I suppose my approach is a bit calculated, but my manners are not, and when you are with a lady for whom you have a very high regard you are not thinking in the least of yourself; you are trying to create around her an atmosphere of ease and graciousness. So that even in America you can achieve something that here is very rare; an attentiveness that will not allow a lady to unfold her own napkin, a realization that her chair must be held by her escort and not by a waiter, so that a captain will deliberately stand back and wait for you to seat your guest instead of, as is usual here even in the best places, holding her chair himself.

He will not attempt to help her off with her coat or wrap, but when you have done it he will be at your elbow to take it, and put it in the cloakroom. And when the wine is brought (a Pontet Canet 1928. I was afraid of that. We get all the bad years here because we don't know the difference), no one is allowed to touch the bottle except the captain who originally conducted you to your table. Rather a farce. But an English lady doesn't realize what a rare thing it is in America for this sort of thing to happen.

There is a lot of Philip Marlowe in that; particularly in the comment about being civil to waiters who are forced to put up with all degrees of rudeness from loud-mouthed racketeers and other undesirables.

The particular delight of getting a letter from Ray was that you never had the least idea what he was going to say next. It might start out with some legal query, but Ray was a writer; the feel of the typewriter under his fingers was all that was needed to set him travelling down the by-ways of thought and comment. 'It might be a good idea to draft a letter to the Inspector of Taxes. His address is Fifth Floor (my God! have they a lift) 229/231 High Holborn.' Or: 'It was pleasant to receive a letter from you after all this time. I was beginning to think you had forgotten my name. Somewhat regretfully I must draw your attention to the fact that twice in your letter you used a singular verb with a plural subject. I had thought this sort of thing tabu in England.' Or: 'I don't terribly care for writing letters to you marked Personal and Private, but I am the soul of indiscretion.' And so he was. And it was the indiscretions, and the asides and the sometimes more serious thoughts about life that made the arrival of the light blue envelope with the dark blue type on it a high point in one solicitor's correspondence.

Ray wrote very little about other authors, and only once at all seriously about himself in his capacity as a writer. He was much interested at this time in the project of writing a stage play. ('I'm tired of mystery stories or perhaps just tired of mine.') The play was to be about the upper middle-class literary and musical set, and would almost certainly have contained speaking likenesses of his friends from this world. Could he have pulled it off? I think the answer must be that, given better health and more writing time, he might well have done it. He had an excellent ear for modes of speech and a considerable technical experience based on his time in Hollywood – a period which produced *Double Indemnity* and *The Blue Dahlia*. From a book by Selwyn Jepson (which he criticized to me rather severely) he rescued one line of dialogue which pleased him a lot. The policeman, 'definitely public school', is accompanying the heroine to a garden party in a taxi. He is correctly attired, in full morning dress and a grey top hat and, in spite of the fact that there is not a cloud in the sky, is carrying a neatly rolled umbrella. When the lady remarks on this he says, sternly: 'It *is* a garden party madam.' ('Ah, the dear English summer.')

On one occasion only did Ray let his hair down about writing. It arose from a mention of his friend Dorothy Gardiner, who had decided to retire from the secretaryship of the Mystery Writers of America, giving as one of her reasons that one or two of the members were 'liable to behave as prima donnas'.

> What the hell makes them get like that? I *always* feel like a beginner when I start a new job. Of course I have been successful, and of course I have made a lot of money, but these things may be largely luck. I don't feel any more important than when I was writing for the pulps. Why should I? Also there is the background that I was a successful business executive, managed eight corporations, and had perhaps the best office staff in Los Angeles, because I knew how to treat them and how to pay them. I don't think these are important talents, but they do make me realize that for a writer to be self-centred or arrogant is just a sign of stupidity. What have we to be arrogant about? One does the best one can at the time, sometimes in very torturing circumstances. Perhaps it is good, perhaps it is bad, but he does his best, and if he has a big success that doesn't make him anything he wasn't before. He still has his neck on the block. He can still flop, or lose his touch. I am the same man I was when I was a struggling nobody. I feel the same. I know more, it is true. I break the rules, and get away with it, but that doesn't make me important.

Ray's third and last visit started on 2 April 1958, beating the start of the tax year by three days. It lasted until 13 August. Time was running out on him. He was drinking far too much, and worrying about it in his sober moments, and drinking some more to oust the worry. To go out with him in the evening was asking for trouble, but he could still be his delightful self at lunch. I have a note that we lunched together at Au Jardin Des Gourmets in Soho on 8 August, less than a week before his return to America. It was a lunch which I shall not forget. Strolling along Dean Street, staring into the window of a photographers' shop which was exhibiting some unusual photographs, I impaled my forehead on the projecting metal cover over a menu outside the restaurant next door. The cut was not serious, but bled a good deal. I staunched it with a handkerchief and pushed on, looking rather more carefully where I was going. Ray was fascinated. He insisted that I had been in a fight with criminals who were upset because they had identified themselves in one of my books. A dangerous place, London. Much worse than San Francisco or Los Angeles. Had not he himself been knocked down in the street and robbed a few weeks before?

By a natural transition the conversation turned to violence in books. I had long held the theory that, in spite of the Biff-Wham-Powee style of strip cartoon narration it was, in fact, more difficult to put across violence convincingly than it was to write a serious and leisurely scene. Ray agreed with this. The average novel reader, he said, doesn't stop very much, or turn back to savour a particular moment. His eye travels very quickly across the page and as the action hots up it travels more quickly still. To make a fight convincing you have to decide precisely where the fighters are standing, how they are holding themselves, and what they plan to do to each other; and then put it across, in nouns and verbs, with a minimum of adjectives and adverbs. Using two bread-rolls, a pepper mill and a mustard pot Ray then demonstrated exactly how he would organize a fight between one goodie and three baddies. 'Always supposing you want the goodies to win, that is. If not, it's much easier, just have him knocked down and kicked in the stomach. But not too often. Violence can get very boring.' I said that two of his acknowledged favourites, Dashiell Hammett and Ian Fleming were fairly free with displays of violence. Ray said they were totally different. 'Hammett was a cop himself. He knew exactly when violence was bound to occur, and inserted it accordingly. Fleming is different. He garnishes his books with violence like you might put a dressing on salad – it's a deliberate extra. Sadistic, but interesting. Maybe that's because he went to Eton.' It was the sort of lunch that goes on and on, until you look up and find that the room is empty and the waiters are ostentatiously laying the other tables for dinner.

That was the last time I saw Ray. The only other documents in the folder are a single letter in January of the following year from La Jolla, still worrying about tax. 'If the accountants cannot work something out to make British tax bearable there's no sense in my coming over to England this year for a few weeks; and I have no desire to live anywhere outside England.' Then a handwritten and almost illegible scrawl, dated '14 February (Late at night)'.

The last document on the file is a copy of the Estate Duty Affidavit, which starts: 'In the Estate of (please use block capitals) RAYMOND THORNTON CHANDLER deceased. Date of death 26 March 1959. Age 70. At 824 Prospect Street, La Jolla, California, USA. Occupation or Description of Deceased: author.'

The Country
Behind The Hill

CLIVE JAMES

I n the long run,' Raymond Chandler writes in *Raymond Chandler Speaking*, 'however little you talk or even think about it, the most durable thing in writing is style, and style is the most valuable investment a writer can make with his time.' At a time when literary values inflate and dissipate almost as fast as the currency, it still looks as if Chandler invested wisely. His style has lasted. A case could be made for saying that nothing else about his books has, but even the most irascible critic or most disillusioned fan (they are often the same person) would have to admit that Chandler at his most characteristic is just that – characteristic and not just quirky. Auden was right in wanting him to be regarded as an artist. In fact Auden's tribute might well have been that of one poet to another. If style is the only thing about Chandler's novels that can't be forgotten, it could be because his style was poetic, rather than prosaic. Even at its most explicit, what he wrote was full of implication. He used to say that he wanted to give a feeling of the country behind the hill.

Since Chandler was already well into middle-age when he began publishing, it isn't surprising that he found his style quickly. Most of the effects that were to mark *The Big Sleep* in 1939 were already present, if only fleetingly, in an early story like 'Killer in the Rain', published in *Black Mask* magazine in 1935. In fact some of the very same sentences are already there. This from 'Killer in the Rain':

> The rain splashed knee-high off the sidewalks, filled the gutters, and big cops in slickers that shone like gun barrels had a lot of fun carrying little girls in silk stockings and cute little rubber boots across the bad places, with a lot of squeezing.

Compare this from *The Big Sleep*:

> Rain filled the gutters and splashed knee-high off the pavement. Big cops in slickers that shone like gun barrels had a lot of fun carrying giggling girls across the bad places. The rain drummed hard on the roof of the car and the burbank top began to leak. A pool of water formed on the floorboards for me to keep my feet in.

So there is not much point in talking about how Chandler's style developed. As soon as he was free of the short-paragraph restrictions imposed by the cheaper pulps, his way of writing quickly found its outer limits: all he needed to do was refine it. The main refining instrument was Marlowe's personality. The difference between the two cited passages is really the difference between John Dalmas and Philip Marlowe. Marlowe's name was not all that more convincing than Dalmas's, but he was a more probable, or at any rate less improbable, visionary. In *The Big Sleep* and all the novels that followed, the secret of plausibility lies in the style, and the secret of the style lies in Marlowe's personality. Chandler once said that he thought of Marlowe as the American mind. As revealed in Chandler's *Notebooks* (edited by Frank MacShane), one of Chandler's many projected titles was *The Man Who Loved the Rain*. Marlowe loved the rain.

Flaubert liked tinsel better than silver because tinsel possessed all silver's attributes plus one in addition – pathos. For whatever reason, Chandler was fascinated by the cheapness of Los Angeles. When he said that it had as much personality as a paper cup, he was saying what he liked about it. When he said that he could leave it without a pang, he was saying why he felt at home there. In a city where the rich were as vulgar as the poor, all the streets were mean. In a democracy of trash, Marlowe was the only aristocrat. Working for twenty-five dollars a day plus expenses (Jim Rockford in the television series *The Rockford Files* now works for ten times that and has to live in a caravan), Marlowe was as free from materialistic constraint as any hermit. He saw essences. Chandler's particular triumph was to find a style for matching Marlowe to the world. Vivid language was the decisive element, which meant that how not to make Marlowe sound like too good a *writer* was the continuing problem. The solution was a kind of undercutting wit, a style in which Marlowe mocked his own fine phrases. A comic style, always on the edge of self-parody – and, of course, sometimes over the edge – but at its best combining the exultant and the sad in an inseparable mixture.

For a writer who is not trying all that hard to be funny, it is remarkable how often Chandler can make you smile. His conciseness can strike you as a kind of wit in itself. The scene with General Sternwood in the hot-house, the set-piece forming chapter two of *The Big Sleep*, is done with more economy than you can remember: there are remarkably few words on the page to generate such a lasting impression of warm fog in the reader's brain. 'The air was thick, wet, steamy and larded with the cloying smell of tropical orchids in bloom.' It's the rogue verb 'larded' which transmits most of the force. Elsewhere, a single simile gives you the idea of General Sternwood's aridity. 'A few locks of dry white hair clung to his scalp, like wild flowers fighting for life on a bare rock.' The fact that he stays dry in the wet air is the measure of General

Sternwood's nearness to death. The bare rock is the measure of his dryness. At their best, Chandler's similes click into place with this perfect appositeness. He can make you laugh, he gets it so right – which perhaps means that he gets it *too* right. What we recognize as wit is always a self-conscious performance.

But since wit that works at all is rare enough, Chandler should be respected for it. And anyway, he didn't always fall into the trap of making his characters too eloquent. Most of Marlowe's best one-liners are internal. In the film of *The Big Sleep*, when Marlowe tells General Sternwood that he has already met Carmen in the hall, he says: 'She tried to sit in my lap while I was standing up.' Bogart gets a big laugh with that line, but only half of the line is Chandler's. All that Chandler's Marlowe says is: 'Then she tried to sit in my lap.' The film version of Marlowe got the rest of the gag from somewhere else – either from William Faulkner, who wrote the movie, or from Howard Hawks, who directed it, or perhaps from both. On the page, Marlowe's gags are private and subdued. About Carmen, he concludes that 'thinking was always going to be a bother to her'. He notices – as no camera could notice, unless the casting director flung his net very wide – that her thumb is like a finger, with no curve in its first joint. He compared the shocking whiteness of her teeth to fresh orange pith. He gets you scared stiff of her in a few sentences.

Carmen is the first in a long line of little witches that runs right through the novels, just as her big sister, Vivian, is the first in a long line of rich bitches who find that Marlowe is the only thing money can't buy. The little witches are among the most haunting of Chandler's obsessions and the rich bitches are among the least. Whether little witch or rich bitch, both kinds of women signal their availability to Marlowe by crossing their legs shortly after sitting down and regaling him with tongue-in-the-lung French kisses a few seconds after making physical contact.

All the standard Chandler character ingredients were there in the first novel, locked in a pattern of action so complicated that not even the author was subsequently able to puzzle it out. *The Big Sleep* was merely the first serving of the mixture as before. But the language was fresh and remains so. When Chandler wrote casually of 'a service station glaring with wasted light' he was striking a note that Dashiell Hammett had never dreamed of. Even the book's title rang a bell. Chandler thought that there were only two types of slang which were any good:

Psychopath Bruno (Robert Walker)
examines the incriminating cigarette lighter
with tennis star Guy (Farley Granger) in
Strangers on a Train, 1950.

The roundabout grinds to a halt – the end of
Bruno in *Strangers on a Train*.

George Sanders and Hans Conreid in *The Falcon Takes Over*, 1942.

ABOVE: Lloyd Nolan as Michael Shayne
with Doris Merrick and Ralph Byrd in *Time
to Kill*, 1942.
OPPOSITE ABOVE: Insurance agent Walter
Neff (Fred MacMurray) and partner in
crime Phyllis Dietrichson (Barbara
Stanwyck) about to claim their *Double
Indemnity* (1944).
BELOW: Claims chief (Edward G. Robinson)
views the dying Walter Neff over his
recorded confession.

ABOVE: Marlowe (Dick Powell) meets the
Grayle family: Claire Trevor, Miles Mander
and Anne Shirley (*Murder, My Sweet*, 1944).
OPPOSITE: The detective in the mirror: the
subjective camera as Philip Marlowe
(Robert Montgomery) inspects new wounds
with femme fatale (Audrey Totter) in *The
Lady in the Lake*, 1946.

ABOVE: Marlowe (Humphrey Bogart) at bay: Marlowe, cigarette in hand, at the mercy of Eddy Mars's thugs.

BELOW: Marlowe victorious, gun in hand, stands over the body of Eddy Mars (*The Big Sleep*, 1946).

slang that had established itself in the language, and slang that you made up yourself. As a term for death, 'the big sleep' was such a successful creation that Eugene O'Neill must have thought it had been around for years, since he used it in *The Iceman Cometh* (1946) as an established piece of low-life tough talk. But there is no reason for disbelieving Chandler's claim to have invented it.

Chandler's knack for slang would have been just as commendable even if he had never invented a thing. As the *Notebooks* reveal, he made lists of slang terms that he had read or heard. The few he kept and used were distinguished from the many he threw away by their metaphorical exactness. He had an ear for depth – he could detect incipient permanence in what sounded superficially like ephemera. A term like 'under glass', meaning to be in prison, attracted him by its semantic compression. In a letter collected in *Raymond Chandler Speaking*, he regards it as self-evident that an American term like 'milk run' is superior to the equivalent British term 'piece of cake'. The superiority being in the range of evocation. As it happened, Chandler *was* inventive, not only in slang but in more ambitiously suggestive figures of speech. He was spontaneous as well as accurate. His second novel, *Farewell, My Lovely* (1940) – which he was always to regard as his finest – teems with showstopping metaphors, many of them dedicated to conjuring up the gargantuan figure of Moose Malloy.

In fact some of them stop the show too thoroughly. When Chandler describes Malloy as standing out from his surroundings like 'a tarantula on a slice of angel food' he is getting things backwards, since the surroundings have already been established as very sordid indeed. Malloy ought to be standing out from them like a slice of angel food on a tarantula. Chandler at one time confessed to Alfred A. Knopf that in *The Big Sleep* he had run his metaphors into the ground, the implication being that he cured himself of the habit later on. But the truth is that he was always prone to overcooking a simile. As Perelman demonstrated in *Farewell, My Lovely Appetizer* (a spoof which Chandler admired), this is one of the areas in which Chandler is most easily parodied, although it should be remembered that it takes a Perelman to do the parodying.

'It was a blonde' says Marlowe, looking at Helen Grayle's photograph, 'a blonde to make a bishop kick a hole in a stained-glass window.' I still laugh when I read that, but you can imagine Chandler jotting down such brain-waves *à propos* of nothing and storing them up against

119

a rainy day. They leap off the page so high that they never again settle back into place, thereby adding to the permanent difficulty of remembering what happens to whom where in which novel. The true wit, in *Farewell, My Lovely* as in all the other books, lies in effects which marry themselves less obtrusively to character, action and setting. Jessie Florian's bathrobe, for example. 'It was just something around her body.' A sentence like that seems hardly to be trying, but it tells you all you need to know. Marlowe's realization that Jessie has been killed – 'The corner post of the bed was smeared darkly with something the flies liked' – is trying harder for understatement, but in those circumstances Marlowe *would* understate the case, so the sentence fits. Poor Jessie Florian. 'She was as cute as a washtub'.

And some of the lines simply have the humour of information conveyed at a blow, like the one about the butler at the Grayle house. As always when Chandler is dealing with Millionaires' Row, the place is described with a cataloguing eye for ritzy detail, as if F. Scott Fitzgerald had written a contribution to *Architectural Digest*. (The Murdock house in *The High Window* bears a particularly close resemblance to Gatsby's mansion: *vide* the lawn flowing 'like a cool green tide around a rock'.) Chandler enjoyed conjuring up the grand houses into which Marlowe came as an interloper and out of which he always went with a sigh of relief, having hauled the family skeletons out of the walk-in cupboards and left the beautiful, wild elder daughter sick with longing for his uncorruptible countenance. But in several telling pages about the Grayle residence, the sentence that really counts is the one about the butler. 'A man in a striped vest and gilt buttons opened the door, bowed, took my hat and was through for the day.'

In the early books and novels, before he moved to Laurel Canyon, when he lived at 615 Cahuenga Buildings on Hollywood Boulevard, near Ivar, telephone Glenview 7537, Marlowe was fond of Los Angeles. All the bad things happened in Bay City. In Bay City there were crooked cops, prostitution, drugs, but after you came to (Marlowe was always coming to in Bay City, usually a long time after he had been sapped, because in Bay City they always hit him very hard) you could drive home. Later on the evil had spread everywhere and Marlowe learned to hate what Los Angeles had become. The set-piece descriptions of his stamping-ground got more and more sour. But the descriptions were always there – one of the strongest threads running through the novels from first to last. And even at their most acridly poisonous they still kept something of the wide-eyed lyricism of that beautiful line in *Farewell, My Lovely* about a dark night in the canyons – the night Marlowe drove Lindsay Marriott to meet his death. 'A yellow window hung here and there by itself, like the last orange.'

There is the usual ration of overcooked metaphors in *The High Window* (1942). Lois Morny gives forth with 'a silvery ripple of laughter that held the unspoiled naturalness of a bubble dance'. (By the time you have worked out that this means her silvery ripple of laughter held no unspoiled naturalness, the notion has gone dead.) We learn that Morny's club in Idle Valley looks like a high-budget musical. 'A lot of light and glitter, a lot of scenery, a lot of clothes, a lot of sound, an all-star cast, and a plot with all the originality and drive of a split fingernail.' Tracing the club through the musical down to the fingernail, your attention loses focus. It's a better sentence than any of Chandler's imitators ever managed, but it was the kind of sentence they felt able to imitate – lying loose and begging to be picked up.

As always, the quiet effects worked better. The back yard of the Morny house is an instant Hockney. 'Beyond was a walled-in garden containing flower-beds crammed with showy annuals, a badminton court, a nice stretch of greensward, and a small tiled pool glittering angrily in the sun.' The rogue adverb 'angrily' is the word that registers the sun's brightness. It's a long step, taken in a few words, to night-time in Idle Valley. 'The wind was quiet out here and the valley moonlight was so sharp that the black shadows looked as if they had been cut with an engraving tool.' Saying how unreal the real looks makes it realer.

'Bunker Hill is old town, lost town, shabby town, crook town.' *The High Window* has many such examples of Chandler widening his rhythmic scope. Yet the best and the worst sentences are unusually far apart. On several occasions Chandler is extraordinarily clumsy. 'He was a tall man with glasses and a high-domed bald head that made his ears look as if they had slipped down his head.' This sentence is literally effortless: the clumsy repetition of 'head' is made possible only because he isn't trying. Here is a useful reminder of the kind of concentration required to achieve a seeming ease. And here is another: 'From the lay of the land a light in the living room ...' Even a writer who doesn't, as Chandler usually did, clean as he goes, would normally liquidate so languorous an alliterative lullaby long before the final draft.

But in between the high points and the low, the general tone of *The High Window* had an assured touch. The narrator's interior monologue is full of the sort of poetry Laforgue liked – *comme ils sont beaux, les trains manqués.* Marlowe's office hasn't changed, nor will it ever. 'The same stuff I had had last year, and the year before that. Not beautiful, not gay, but better than a tent on the beach.' Marlowe accuses the two cops, Breeze and Spangler, of talking dialogue in which every line is a punch-line. Criticism is not disarmed: in Chandler, everybody talks that kind of dialogue most of the time. But the talk that matters most is the talk going on inside Marlowe's head, and Chandler was making it more subtle with each book.

Chandler's descriptive powers are at their highest in *The Lady in the Lake* (1943). It takes Marlowe a page and half of thoroughly catalogued natural detail to drive from San Bernardino to Little Fawn Lake, but when he gets there he sees the whole thing in a sentence. 'Beyond the gate the road wound for a couple of hundred yards through trees and then suddenly below me was a small oval lake deep in trees and rocks and wild grass, like a drop of dew caught in a curled leaf.' Hemingway could do bigger things, but small moments like those were Chandler's own. (Nevertheless Hemingway got on Chandler's nerves: Dolores Gonzales in *The Little Sister* is to be heard saying: 'I was pretty good in there, no?' and the nameless girl who vamps Marlowe at Roger Wade's party in *The Long Goodbye* spoofs the same line. It should be remembered, however, that Chandler admired Hemingway to the end, forbearing to pour scorn even on *Across The River And Into The Trees.* (The digs at Papa in Chandler's novels can mainly be put down to self-defence.)

The Little Sister (1949). Chandler's first post-war novel, opens with Marlowe stalking a bluebottle fly around his office. 'He didn't want to sit down. He just wanted to do wing-overs and sing the prologue to *Pagliacci.*' Ten years before, in 'Trouble is My Business' John Dalmas felt like singing the same thing after being sapped in Harriet Huntress's apartment. Chandler was always ready to bring an idea back for a second airing. A PhD thesis could be written about the interest Marlowe takes in bugs and flies. There is another thesis in the tendency of Chandler's classier dames to show a startling line of white scalp in the parting of their hair: Dolores Gonzales, who throughout *The Little Sister* propels herself at Marlowe like Lupe Velez seducing Errol Flynn, is only one of several high-toned vamps possessing this tonsorial feature. 'She made a couple of drinks in a couple of glasses you could almost have stood umbrellas in.' A pity about that 'almost' – it ruins a good hyperbole.

Moss Spink's extravagance is better conveyed: 'He waved a generous hand on which a canary-yellow diamond looked like an amber traffic light.'

But as usual the would-be startling images are more often unsuccessful than successful. The better work is done lower down the scale of excitability. Joseph P. Toad, for example. 'The neck of his canary-yellow shirt was open wide, which it had to be if his neck was going to get out.' Wit like that lasts longer than hyped-up similes. And some of the dialogue, though as stylized as ever, would be a gift to actors: less supercharged than usual, it shows some of the natural balance which marked the lines Chandler had been writing for the movies. Here is Marlowe sparring with Sheridan Ballou.

'Did she suggest how to go about shutting my mouth?'
'I got the impression she was in favour of doing it with some kind of heavy blunt instrument.'

Such an exchange is as playable as anything in *Double Indemnity* or *The Blue Dahlia*. And imagine what Laird Cregar would have done with Toad's line 'You could call me a guy what wants to help out a guy that don't want to make trouble for a guy.' Much as he would have hated the imputation, Chandler's toil in the salt-mines under the Paramount mountain had done things for him. On the other hand, the best material in *The Little Sister* is inextricably bound up with the style of Marlowe's perception, which in turn depends on Chandler's conception of himself. There could be no complete screen rendition of the scene with Jules Oppenheimer in the studio patio. With peeing dogs instead of hot-house steam, it's exactly the same lay-out as Marlowe's encounter with General Sternwood in *The Big Sleep*, but then there was no filming *that* either. The mood of neurotic intensity – Marlowe as the soldier-son, Sternwood/Oppenheimer as the father-figure at death's door – would be otiose in a film script, which requires that all action be relevant. In the novels, such passages are less about Marlowe than about Chandler working out his obsessions through Marlowe, and nobody ever wanted to make a film about Chandler.

In *The Long Goodbye* (1953) Marlowe moves to a house on Yucca Avenue in Laurel Canyon and witnesses the disintegration of Terry Lennox. Lennox can't control his drinking. Marlowe, master of his own thirst, looks sadly on. As we now know, Chandler in real life was more Lennox than Marlowe. In the long dialogues between these two characters he is really talking to himself. There is no need to be afraid of the biographical fallacy: even if we knew nothing about Chandler's life, it would still be evident that a fantasy is being worked out. Worked out but not admitted – as so often happens in good–bad books, the author's obsessions are being catered to, not examined. Chandler, who at least worked for a living, had reason for thinking himself more like Marlowe than like Lennox. (Roger Wade, the other of the book's big drinkers, is, being a writer, a bit closer to home.) Nevertheless Marlowe is a day-dream – more and more of a day-dream as Chandler gets better and better at making him believable. By this time it's Marlowe v. the Rest of the World. Of all Chandler's nasty cops, Captain Gregorius is the nastiest. 'His big nose was a network of burst capillaries'; but even in the face of the ultimate nightmare Marlowe keeps his nerve. Nor is he taken in by Eileen Wade, superficially the dreamiest of all Chandler's dream girls.

It was a close-run thing, however, Chandler mocked romantic writers who always used three adjectives but Marlowe fell into the same habit when contemplating Eileen Wade. 'She looked exhausted now, and frail, and very beautiful.' Perhaps he was tipped off when Eileen suddenly caught the same disease and started referring to 'the wild, mysterious, improbable kind of love that never comes but once'. In the end she turns out to be a killer, a dream-girl gone sour like Helen Grayle in *Farewell, My Lovely*, whose motherly clutch ('smooth and soft and warm and comforting') was that of a strangler. *The Long Goodbye* is the book of Marlowe's irretrievable disillusion.

> I was as hollow and empty as the spaces between the stars. When I got home I mixed a stiff one and stood by the open window in the living-room and sipped it and listened to the ground swell of the traffic on Laurel Canyon Boulevard and looked at the glare of the big, angry city hanging over the shoulder of the hills through which the boulevard had been cut. Far off the banshee wail of police or fire sirens rose and fell, never for very long completely silent. Twenty-four hours a day somebody is running, somebody else is trying to catch him.

Even Marlowe got caught. Linda Loring nailed him. 'The tip of her tongue touched mine.' His vestal virginity was at long last ravished away. But naturally there was no Love, at least not yet.

Having broken the ice, Marlowe was to be laid again, most notably by the chic, leg-crossing Miss Vermilyea in Chandler's next novel, *Play-*

back (1958). It is only towards the end of that novel that we realize how thoroughly Marlowe is being haunted by Linda Loring's memory. Presumably this is the reason why Marlowe's affair with Miss Vermilyea is allowed to last only one night. ('I hate you,' she said with her mouth against mine. 'Not for this, but because perfection never comes twice and with us it came too soon. And I'll never see you again and I don't want to. It would have to be for ever or not at all.') We presume that Miss Vermilyea wasn't just being tactful.

Anyway, Linda Loring takes the prize, but not before Marlowe has raced through all his usual situations, albeit in compressed form. Once again, for example, he gets hit on the head. 'I went zooming out over a dark sea and exploded in a sheet of flame.' For terseness this compares favourably with an equivalent moment in 'Bay City Blues', written twenty years before:

> Then a naval gun went off in my ear and my head was a large pink firework exploding into the vault of the sky and scattering and falling slow and pale, and then dark, into the waves. Blackness ate me up.

Chandler's prose had attained respectability, but by now he had less to say with it – perhaps because time had exposed his day-dreams to the extent that even he could see them for what they were. The belief was gone. In *The Poodle Springs Mystery*, his last, unfinished novel Marlowe has only one fight left to fight, the war against the rich. Married now to Linda, he slugs it out with her toe to toe. It is hard to see why he bothers to keep up the struggle. Even heroes get tired and not even the immortal stay young forever. Defeat was bound to come some time and although it is undoubtedly true that the rich are corrupt at least Linda knows how corruption ought to be done: the classiest of Chandler's classy dames, the richest bitch of all, she will bring Marlowe to a noble downfall. There is nothing vulgar about Linda. (If that Hammond organ-*cum*-cocktail bar in their honeymoon house disturbs you, don't forget that the place is only rented.)

So Marlowe comes to an absurd end, and indeed it could be said that he was always absurd. Chandler was always dreaming. He dreamed of being more attractive than he was, taller than he was, less trammelled than he was, braver than he was. But so do most men. We dream about our ideal selves, and it is at least arguable that we would be even less ideal if we didn't. Marlowe's standards of conduct would be our standards if we had his courage. We can rationalize the discrepancy by convincing ourselves that if we haven't got his courage he hasn't got our mortgage, but the fact remains that his principles are real.

Marlowe can be hired, but he can't be bought. As a consequence, he is alone. Hence his lasting appeal. Not that he is without his repellent aspects. His race prejudice would amount to outright fascism if it were not so evident that he would never be able to bring himself to join a movement. His sexual imagination is deeply suspect and he gets hit on the skull far too often for someone who works largely with his head. His taste in socks is oddly vile for one who quotes so easily from Browning ('the poet, not the automatic'). But finally you recognize his tone of voice.

It is your own, day-dreaming of being tough, of giving the rich bitch the kiss-off, of saying smart things, of defending the innocent, of being the hero. It is a silly day-dream because anyone who could really do such splendid things would probably not share it, but without it the rest of us would be even more lost than we are. Chandler incarnated this necessary fantasy by finding a style for it. His novels are exactly as good as they should be. In worse books, the heroes are too little like us: in better books, too much.

His Own
Long Goodbye

NATASHA SPENDER

A few months after the death of his wife, and a few weeks after his own first suicide attempt, Raymond Chandler arrived in England and settled into the Connaught Hotel, sixty-seven years old, still suicidal, ill, very alcoholic and absorbed in what he always called the 'long nightmare' of mourning. Knowing nothing then of this recent history, I found myself one day in late April 1955 sitting next to an elderly American gentleman at luncheon in the house of his publisher Hamish Hamilton. I saw only the lumbering courtesy and humour, which he seemed to force through an aura of despair to respond to the cheerful kindly conversation of his hostess. After luncheon when Yvonne Hamilton had told me the story, I tentatively suggested inviting him, which she encouraged me to do, though I supposed that he might well be in no mood for social life. However, he responded with apparent pleasure and gruff grace to my invitation for dinner in the following week, 'as long as there aren't any literary heavyweights around'. Hardly wishing to conduct a weighing-in of our friends, we invited younger non-literary ones, whom we knew to be intelligent enthusiasts for his books.

It was an amusing evening; he seemed delighted by compliments, and even rather exhilarated to deliver himself, with a certain flourish, of a far too deprecating reply. It seemed touching that, to quote Adlai Stevenson, he should allow himself to 'inhale some of the flattery' with a mixture of modesty and swagger, as if a long-immured hermit should be eagerly overjoyed at anyone even remembering his name. In his letter of thanks – which characteristically arrived by special messenger – he said that his hostess might be thought 'a rather over-enthusiastic appraiser of lowdown literature. I must insist that I am nothing but a glib and "quick-brained" character who chanced on a formula that would permit almost infinite experiment into the American vernacular.' Yet in spite of the pace of all our gaiety, and his sudden flights of glorious nonsense, his great brooding silences and the shadow of his desperation had hung in the air. Later, one of the guests, Jocelyn Rickards, talked to me of the alarm we both felt concerning his survival. She believed that his gentlemanly good manners would never permit him to implement his evidently strong suicidal impulses if he had an imminent social engagement with a lady. So in turn we each invited ourselves to a meal with him, or him to one with us, other friends joined in, and so began the 'shuttle service' by which our small group tried to ensure that he was never out of sight of an impending gentle and undemanding social engagement, and that he could at bad times telephone one of us at any time in the twenty-four hours.

Those telephone calls in the small hours (for he was particularly insomniac after his wife's death) could start out as long stretches of silence broken only by heavy breathing, followed by grim battles of his nihilism versus our spirit, but sooner or later he might be coaxed into feeling that there was not long to wait for the festivities of the following day; or his sardonic mockery of one's efforts to encourage him led to his being unable to resist making a joke, and then sudden delight at his own sally brought with it a resurgence of pleasure and hopefulness; he would ring off chuckling with triumph at having got the best of an argument and no doubt happily thinking up further volleys to shoot off at luncheon. Sometimes 'Hang on till breakfast-time' was the only way to deal with those early morning calls if all else failed, and then one or other of us would go to breakfast with him – 'The Dawn Patrol' as Alison Hooper called it.

The nucleus of the shuttle service was Jocelyn Rickards, Alec Murray, Alison Hooper and the Spenders. Others joined in, but some dropped out fairly quickly because of the 'emotional blackmail' he used in his suicidal state. Our motivation (as mine continued to be to the end, having been the last survivor of that group to continue responsibility) was to see him through to a point when he would want to go on living; where he could recognize and accept reality without its disrupting the fantasy into which all his psychic energy had been channelled when he was writing his novels; and above all where he would reverse the process of slowly killing himself with drink. But alternating with extremely alcoholic behaviour, his fantasy seemed entirely to be used in acting out romantic Don Quixote illusions, from the untoward effects of which we tried gently to deliver him, though at times it seemed far from easy or even advisable to do so, for the process would make him very ruffled. As we came to know him better, and to answer the many suicide threats or cries for help which seemed at one and the same time to be absolutely genuine, yet elaborately staged, it became no easier to judge the degree of his desperation, for you can't take chances with suicide, and any accompanying play-acting doesn't guarantee that the intention is less serious. So, as Alison remembers, if telephoned with the peremptory 'Unless you can get here in half-an-hour you'll find a mess like strawberry jam on the sidewalk', one was there in half-an-hour – though sometimes one might arrive to find a totally silent abstracted figure wrapped in gloom. The oscillation of his mood between exuberance and despair made one realize he was having a concealed nervous breakdown, concealed in that he could put up a good superficial show on social occasions, but in private he was resolutely and scornfully impervious to our suggestions that he consult medical advice for these extreme episodes. Indeed, he put up a very good show with us when he was in the mood, charming, considerate and wonderfully funny – 'sparkle' was one of his favourite words, and when he found his vein of good humour, it could be a Catherine-wheel display.

At first we didn't realize how muffled anxiety existed even at the cosy and undemanding social evenings he had in our company in ones or twos. At the Connaught, he would roll into the bar like a tough old Hemingway returning from a lonely battle at sea, he would hurl his order for 'gimlets' at the barman, and then slump flabbily into a chair – his gestures too expansive, his voice rather loud, the topic too boastful until, after a time, he began to feel more at ease. Our judicious delaying of more orders for drinks, combining with his increasing feeling of safety in the company of friends, brought out a gentler humour, yet curiously dissociated from what we knew to be his true state of mind. However, in both despairing and exuberant phases he seemed propelled by anxiety. Those virtuoso verbal improvisations at luncheon at the Connaught which, by their elegant outrageousness, both shocked and entranced the neighbours at the next tables into abandoning all pretence of attending to their own conversations, gave the impression that he was wound up to concert pitch, and after such cadenzas were over he was quite exhausted. (Later, under the title 'A Routine to Shock the Neighbours', he tried to write out some pieces in the same vein, but they emerged on paper as flat, laboured and sometimes, in their oddly automatic tone of 'porn', rather embarrassing.)

In his despairing times too, his anxiety rose as he talked of his wife's death, and it then seemed strange to us that *after* a traumatic loss a person could seem anxious rather than sad, almost as if still in anticipation of the shock. His imaginary misapprehensions about the circumstances of our lives were also at times suffused with unnecessary anxiety. I remember a whole luncheon taken up with his unrealistic fears for Jocelyn's safety during a two-week absence of her flat-mate, though Eaton Square was an eminently safe district in those days; furthermore, she had a wide circle of friends, and being of an independent temperament spent her days happily painting in her studio. But he clung obstinately to visions of a violent burglary or waylaying in spite of all reassurances.

We all attributed this evident anxiety to the recent events which had made him so suicidal, and no doubt they had made things worse. But as we came to know his life-history it was clear that he had always had an anxious temperament. His mother had divorced his drunken and violent father, taking her seven-year-old son to England to live with her mother and sister in Dulwich – in a middle-class household of high Victorian rectitude, where they were made to feel like disgraced poor relations. Raymond always talked of his father as a 'swine', his mother as a 'saint', and of his own schooldays at Dulwich College with pride for his intellectual prowess, particularly as a classical scholar, and for his character of exceptional sexual purity. The self-control of the Arnold tradition, mingled with the chaste and deathladen-images of the Tennysonian Arthurian legends which inspired his own early poetry, was a dominant influence throughout his life, despite his migration to themes of Californian violence, sexual freedom, and corruption. From his reminiscences it seemed clear that at far too early an age he was made to feel that he was 'the man of the family' in this household of women, at the same time protecting his mother and sharing the humiliations she suffered from the moralizing condescension of his aunt and grandmother. Clinically this pattern of childhood situations is often recognized as a determining factor for later homosexuality. By his own account this was not so in Raymond's case, though its strenuous repression might have accounted for the alert and vehement aversion he always went out of his way to express towards it. This may be why we all, without a second thought, assumed that he was a repressed homosexual, too facile a conclusion perhaps, but backed up by the fact that for all the jolly talk he didn't ever make the slightest advance to any of us nor to any of our friends. But then also he had seemed from his first arrival to be a psychological and physical wreck, who aroused only our maternal compassion.

In the cold moralistic atmosphere of the Dulwich household he could hardly have failed to acquire a self-punishing conscience so that he was not only anxious, but also anxious to succeed, to gain approval. Traces of his need for maternal approval remained in his demeanour in old age, for I remember one afternoon at a swimming pool in Palm Springs when after each dive he made, he would come to where Evelyn Hooker and I were stretched out on chaises-longues, like two dowagers doing our embroidery, and would stand waiting until we told him what a fine dive it had been. As a schoolboy his strong desire for achievement was rewarded with academic success; for him as for many writers, his mastery of words gave him a sense of power. Pleasure in the demands of literary craftsmanship seems to go with a certain temperament (the obsessional defence), for the written word, unlike the human being, can't hit back. How interesting that in a life so lonely and bare of lasting friendships, some of his most enduring and rewarding ones were with pen-pals, a 'safer' form of communication, for the delay of reply provided a cushioning of impact. His correspondence with Hamish Hamilton, which was a source of great amusement and pleasure to them both, had lasted well over a decade before they ever met.

His rigid use of his own idiosyncratic moral judgments as a stick to beat others with was part of that same powerful self-punishing super-ego with which he strove for perfection of the life (perforce secluded) and of the work, and from which struggle his only refuge was the bottle. It made him feel anxious and 'threatened' if he realized that there was opposition to his code, which was then energetically used to destroy the reality of other people's, with accusations of 'sham', 'hypocrisy', 'snobbery', or whatever. This persecution from within was kept at bay by projection and denial of reality in fantasy, which suggests that Chandler may have had to pay a very high price for the novels we enjoy.

Sustained compassion he felt for those whom he could regard totally as 'victims' to be rescued; about more fortunate people, though with ordinary problems and human failings, he could often be scathing and censorious. He was generally courteous and gentle to women, and liked to see himself as their active protector, but what he really sought was their protection in the helpless condition to which illness had so dismayingly reduced him. When this need made him at times as demanding as an anxious bullying child, one wondered how much the idolized saintly mother had given to him of the warmth and reassurance he had needed in childhood. It appeared that he had always tried, amidst dangers, to win the approval of his elders, and valiantly to protect her, the first 'victim' or even martyr perhaps? One doesn't know. He used to regret her never having remarried (as *she* put it, for *his* sake); he himself had not regarded possibly acquiring a step-father as the hazardous step she saw it to be. He lived with her until she died of cancer when he was in his mid-thirties. Like D.H. Lawrence he had to contend with her total disapproval during her terminal illness, and two weeks after

132

her death he married Cissy who was then still a beautiful woman, in her mid-fifties, much nearer to his mother's age than to his own. They led a devoted and for long stretches of time secluded life until her death in her eighties, after a long illness. They were of course childless. We knew from people who had met them a few years earlier that they had both seemed nervy and lost on their first visit to London, she very ailing, he very protective towards her. Though knowing his social nerves one wonders if even then his refusal to dine out without her was not partly for the maternal moral support he still both needed and found in her company. His own reminiscences of her were adoring, irresistibly lyrical and full of delight at Cissy's exploits which showed her spirit and charm – she managed on one occasion to drive the car right over an irate policeman's foot, not once, but again in reverse, yet even then beguiling him into such instant and helpless admiration as to allow her to escape unbooked.

He would recall the rugged struggle for existence of their early marriage. There followed a swift rise to power and riches in the oil business attributed to his own 'toughness' (a favourite epithet of approbation possibly arising out of childhood – 'identification with the aggressor' – since he had in fact been a sensitive and not very strong child, always the introverted intellectual, never the fantasized extroverted Marlowe type). He recalled the privations Cissy loyally shared during his late ten-year apprenticeship as a mystery writer, and again the uncompromising 'toughness' with which he outsmarted the villains and fought his way to success through the corruption and shifting sands of Hollywood, where he had made the fortune of which he was now so openly proud, and which in his present euphoric phases he seemed to be generously jettisoning just as, in his despair, he was jettisoning his life.

What we didn't know until somewhat later was that both his oil business and his Hollywood careers had ended in débâcles of alcoholism, though he always presented different explanations, denying to himself the true reason for his failures: his inability to cope with colleagues, and the contrast between their invigorating uninhibited social life and the isolation of his marriage, retreat into which provided a therapeutic setting for recovery from these disasters. A healing maternal presence in the home left him free to pursue the interior monologue of fantasy which went into his writing, and even through the agony and apprehension of Cissy's last illness it provided an escape from intense strain.

He wrote *The Long Goodbye* as Cissy lay dying, and we who tried to see him through the subsequent 'long nightmare' recognize in the book three distinct self-portraits. It may well reflect the interior dialogues between facets of his own personality as he looked back upon their long life together, which he was soon to lose. Afterwards his London conversations so strikingly resembled the dialogue of all three characters in turn that one feels his endeavour to impose fictional roles upon us also was part of this urgent involuntary bid for American continuity amid the bewildering though enjoyable impact of an alien English style. Troubled memories of gruelling tests of nerve in the 1914–18 war were frequently followed by patriotic approval of the immense current military strength of America.

Like Terry Lomax, Raymond was a young ex-soldier in the early twenties, battle-scarred and scared, whose pride was that 'of a man who has nothing else'. Lomax, when castigated by Philip Marlowe for being a moral defeatist, says that his life is all 'an act'. Raymond often acknowledged his own tendency to fantasize and play-act, and once wrote to me in apology for having distorted the truth: 'I have such an endless sense of the dramatic that I never seem to play any part quite straight. My wife always said I should have been an actor.' To an American friend, referring to his two London visits which, possibly out of pride, he had presented as romantically spectacular when in truth they had been consumed in mourning, he wrote 'All the rest has been play-acting'.

Like that of Roger Wade, the successful, middle-aged, alcoholic and egocentric writer, Raymond's drunken stream of consciousness could also at bad moments be full of self-hatred, writer's angst and sarcastic hostility. Wade says: 'I have a lovely wife who loves me, and a lovely publisher who loves me, and I love me best of all.' Wade's wife echoes Cissy in saying 'He was a good actor – most writers are.' Like Raymond himself, Wade is childless and says: 'If I had a ten-year-old kid, which God forbid, the brat would be asking me "What are you running away from when you drink, Daddy?"'

Again in apology Raymond wrote to me of himself: 'It's as if I had two natures, one good, one bad . . . A man who's been an alcoholic and has lived all his life in the shadow of an alcoholic father (even if he never saw him) so much so that he was glad he could not have children – they might be tainted – can never rid himself of the contempt for his failings which that ensures, and that sometimes, however wrongly, he transfers to others who do not in any way deserve it.'

Marlowe of course, represents Chandler's ideal self, the conscience which punished the Roger Wade within him though not without commendation for achievement (for Wade in the book is 'a bit of a bastard and maybe a bit of a genius too'), and befriended the Terry Lomax within, not without censure. Marlowe describes this friendship by saying 'You bought a lot of me Terry', and another time 'I owned a piece of him I had invested time and money in him.' This ticking taximeter of money at the heart of it seems a forlornly mistrustful attitude to friendship, poignantly so, considering Raymond's generosity. In Marlowe's brief love affair with the millionairess Linda Loring the taximeter ticks through the dialogue on the credit side, and in the unfinished novel *The Poodle Springs Mystery* Marlow marries Linda, seemingly alert to the dangers of being morally defeated as Terry had been by her sister's money. But we shall never know how it might have ended.

All three characters were drinkers, like Raymond himself, two of them disintegrating and despairing, for only the ideal-self Marlowe shows a disposition towards integrity. As aspects of Raymond's own character their dominance veered with his mood, Roger Wade his 'bad self', Philip Marlowe his 'good self' and Terry Lomax his anxious one. These three, often in conflict, were in good times subordinated to a fourth, the genial, generous and benevolently paternal friend.

He used to seek our admiration for the 'Hemingway–Rockefeller–Bogart' persona he projected from his past, yet he little knew that though his new 'girl-friends', as he was pleased to call us, found that image entertaining if only partly credible, we truly admired him for quite a different sort of valour. For his was a grief more protracted, agonizing, and complex than that which he described, and his battle for survival was more profound than he himself seemed to realize. Indeed, although by care or good luck we got him through his suicidal episodes, his slow alcoholic suicide continued, except for short periods of vigilant care, until his death, a little over four years after that of Cissy.

At the outset, we were too confident that his oscillations between euphoria and helpless suicidal gloom were no more than the temporary derangement consequent on bereavement. We thought only time was needed to end them. Raymond confided to Jocelyn during their first luncheon that he didn't have long to live as he had incurable cancer of the throat. After a tussle she persuaded him to consult a Harley Street physician, we saw him into the Westminster Hospital, whence after a few days he emerged with the diagnosis of smoker's laryngitis and a determination to ignore all instructions. After considerable provocation the distinguished physician withdrew politely from all responsibility for his wayward uncooperative patient; this being the first of many such relationships Raymond was to have but not to hold with English doctors. Who on earth could have persuaded him to seek psychiatric help, for he certainly wasn't a docile patient? Alison and I used to consult a friend Dr John Thompson (later of the Albert Einstein Hospital) as to how our friendly but unprofessional help could be most effective, but since it *was* only amateur, all one can say is that it was probably better than nothing. Soon afterwards there was liver trouble and a host of minor ailments, through all of which we nursed him or saw him into hospital, trying (when liver tests required *total* abstinence) to extract the carefully hidden whisky bottles from his luggage without his spotting us.

What we admired was the courage and sporadic humour with which (even amid the egocentric self-pity) he fought his way through these alarming roller-coaster changes of mood, the plunging into loneliness and illness, the zooming up into deliciously irresistible sagas of outrageous nonsense; the bullying contentiousness swivelling suddenly to the disarming repartee, and all as if it was happening to him entirely outside of his control. Though he could at times be an intolerable crosspatch, we admired the courage (sometimes very dramatized courage) with which he undertook those gruesome drying-out cures, and the effort he often generously made to break out of his hopelessness in order to entertain us. Impossible as he could sometimes be, we all became fond of him.

Raymond's conversation swung with his mood. It ranged from the brilliantly fantastic to the serious, contentious or moralizing (for there were times when he found it impossible to be unreservedly appreciative of *anybody*, even his 'best friends'). At other times he would remain morose or sunk in silence. After which perhaps he might on rare occasions talk quietly of Cissy and his whole past life without the usual sentiment or pantomime, and about his reasons for refusing adamantly to admit that he had a future. These occasions were rare for he was a fantasist, so much so that it was often quite difficult to tell whether some story of exploits had not first been improvised and then congealed into permanent credence by frequent repetition. These stories would even sometimes be about one of us. We heard them with indulgent amazement at the kaleidoscopic change a perfectly ordinary event had undergone, emerging as dramatic or amusing with sometimes only a slender thread connecting it with the truth.

As far as we could see, he made no attempt to work in the first two years after Cissy's death and symptomatically his only publications were a letter to a newspaper to protest about the death of a woman by hanging, and an article (also for a newspaper) on his feelings about Cissy's death. But the fantasy which in health and seclusion had gone into novels, in this period of illness and disorientation in a strange country (for his homecoming to England had been unexpectedly fraught with culture-shock) was either acted out in extravaganzas of social behaviour or found its way into letters, of which he must have written hundreds. If one knew him well, one could winnow fact from fantasy in his letters, but since they read as plausibly as his novels it is impossible to imagine how a stranger would ever be able to do so. Although some parts were lucid, benevolent and even brilliantly reasoned, friends told me that they more or less ignored other parts of them as alcoholic distortion, or, as I did, 'let it ride', interpreting their exaggerated accounts of people, whether approving or scurrilous, as symptoms of his disorientation and misery. Like Roger Wade, he seemed to be able to type equally well, whether sober or drunk.

His legacy from childhood of Victorian values was merely modified, not eliminated, by changes in his environment. They contributed to his deep distrust and disbelief in the generosity of human nature; people are always out to get something out of you and 'toughness' is the only weapon against corruption. This legacy was manifest in his repertoire of pejorative epithets. '*Snobbery*' – yet he himself had vestiges of that Victorian middle-class attitude: 'Tradesmen come in by the back door'. He was too impressed by English titles ('blue blood' as he called it) and great family fortunes. '*Literary Pretentiousness*' – he was always ready with suspicion of possible condescension towards the 'mystery writer', particularly that of any other writer whose classical education might be better than his own and, in addition, whose liberation from Victorian values might give him more intellectual adventurousness with new theories than Raymond's rigid ethic left him free to enjoy. '*Sham and Hypocrisy*' – his sometimes harsh judgments of others were, one felt, also part of this legacy.

There were various perennial characters in his more elated fantasy conversation, all of whom could be understood as representing some anxiety of his (clearly related to this repertoire of pejorative epithets or to his hatred of his own Roger Wade alcoholism) which was allayed by the fantasy. For instance, there was the 'posh doctor' in striped trousers, whose urbanity or superiority were both mocked yet regarded as formidable; he was hated for 'having too much on the ball'. (Striped trousers were not only formal attire for Harley Street consultants in 1955, but in his youth in England an authoritative figure of a publishing house, also clad in striped trousers, had 'thrown him out', insulting him by suggesting he write cheap serial stories for a living, upon which Raymond had left England for ever.) The 'posh doctor' was always eclipsing Raymond in worldliness, success with women, money, and suavity of manners, and above all was always being condescendingly stringent, issuing warnings or challenges about Raymond's excessive drinking. But in these various fantasy encounters Raymond always got the best of it in the end with some brilliantly delivered insult, after which he would leave the 'posh doctor' with sagging jaw, and go on his way laughing.

There was an English 'duke' in his garden as magnificent as Kew, whose quietly-voiced, politely phrased rebukes to Raymond for his crude and racy American conversation would at first seem humiliating, but finally Raymond would lay a sophisticated verbal trap, the duke would falter and fall headlong, the duchess would gaze in admiration, and Raymond would stroll away refusing all invitations brought by the footman who was sent hurrying after him.

Sometimes a fantasy figure was superimposed upon a real person to whom it bore not even a superficial resemblance, and it was utterly useless to protest about the transformation. Such a one was Cyril Connolly, who as a literary figure also had 'too much on the ball'. In fact, Raymond had been excessively grumpy the only time he was invited to Ian Fleming's house in Victoria Square precisely because we had all talked a little (but to his mind too much) of the pleasures of knowing Cyril who was in fact a brilliant classical scholar who had read more widely than Raymond, and whose conversation and writing could be a cornucopia of these treasures, together with surprising wit, instant parody, sharp aphorism. To Raymond our admiration of Connolly made him suspect him (quite wrongly) of despising a 'mystery writer'. 'Cyril Connolly' appeared in Raymond's fantasy as a curious mixture of hedonistic dilettante yet pedantic and censorious critic who knew nothing of the 'real' world of violence (nor of course did Raymond in his very secluded life) and who when finding himself in an alarming situation requiring instant tough physical action would be left helpless and gasping, whilst Raymond would stride in and master the whole dangerous predicament in a matter of minutes. This fantasy of

Chandler's physical invincibility was particularly sad when one looked at the sick and shaky man who was entertaining one with these stories, the whole image having arisen out of a single moment of annoyance at feeling socially neglected.

Though, in fact, at that luncheon he had been very much the centre of attention. He had arrived pointing a finger of triumph at Ian and crowing, 'You *forgot* the glass of water. He had just read *Diamonds Are Forever*, prided himself on detecting all faults of detail, and was referring to the omission, in a scene at a short-order counter in Las Vegas, of the first object always to be placed before the customer; and Ian had amiably deferred to the colleague he so admired, and to whom he inscribed a book 'To Field Marshal Chandler from Private Ian Fleming'.

But, as often happens with alcoholics, Raymond was capable of seizing upon some chance remark of a person he hardly knew, brooding upon it, and transposing it into his own private fictional context, which then wholly determined his subsequent attitude towards that person. On the other hand he could be fiercely loyal to a friend if anyone else made what he thought to be an unjust or 'caddish' comment, never forgotten and forever held against the speaker, however unconsidered (and subsequently withdrawn) the remark may have been. At other times he could change his opinion within days, 'that slimy punk' having become 'that sweet sad man' or vice versa. He had a very clear eye for details but not for the realities of the lives around him; his novelist's selection and manipulation were always at work to fashion the characters he projected from within.

Another perennial fantasy/real-life composite figure who used to appear as an imaginary protagonist was the rich father of one of his 'girl-friends' whom Raymond, never having met him, imagined as a Harlan Potter. He would in imagination rehearse a session of hard bargaining which used to begin by the august and icy 'Mr Potter' saying: 'I can't put it out of my mind. Mr Chandler, that you wish to marry my daughter for her money'... 'That is certainly a factor.' Chandler would reply; after which with all royalty figures at his fingertips he would point out how much he was worth, and so on, reminiscent of his stories of his 'brutal bargaining with Hollywood moguls'. He himself later realized that this scene related to his inability to work during this time and fears about his continued earning power since he was very keen to lead a life of secure stylish luxury.

Later in May he moved from the Connaught to a spacious apartment overlooking the trees in Eaton Square, which Alison had found and helped him to arrange, though he was quite obstreperous about her suggestions for making it more comfortable. There must have been times when our help reminded him too sharply of his loss, for Cissy had been very fond of rearranging furniture. It was near to Jocelyn and to Alec Murray, also not far from Helga Greene, a new friend who also gave him as much attention as she could amid a busy life. For the next few weeks Eaton Square life became an amazing succession of contrasts: troughs of illness and misery, crests of exuberant festive gestures. After one of our all-day vigils by rota when he had been particularly ill and irritable, he could be suddenly jubilant or contrite, and lavish presents would appear – whole sprays of orchids to Jocelyn, red roses to me, or (most endearing, as Alison said) the four-page letter of apology typed in the small hours and sent by special messenger if his deportment and contentiousness had been, as he would own, intolerable, and he was afraid he had tried his friends too far.

He alternated not only in mood but also between a clear idea of his friends' desire to help and compulsions to test out their staying power by provoking them with intentionally outrageous behaviour into, as he thought and very much feared, *possibly* deserting him. Sometimes he would totally ignore the 'only flowers or chocolates' rule and a box from a jeweller arrived and would be sent back to the shop. However he could on certain occasions become quite distraught no matter how tactfully one declined, and it became useless and even unkind to argue. Then we accepted happily, realizing that these lavish gestures were both pure gratitude and the fantasy of his novels rolled into one.

During a particularly bad bout of his illness, Jocelyn and I concealed from him that I was to play a concerto with the Bournemouth Symphony Orchestra since he was far too shaky to go. However he somehow had found out and when, after the concert was over, and a dinner with the mayor and council was in progress in the vast and otherwise deserted dining room of a large hotel, Raymond suddenly arrived white-faced and ghostly in full evening dress with white silk scarf, lurched towards the table and said he'd come to take me back to London. Lady Groves, who already knew from me a little of our patient's history and present plight, persuaded him to join us, and after dinner he was helped, almost carried, by the conductor Stanford Robinson to the waiting car – a very upright and ancient Rolls Royce the floor of which was covered with silver ice buckets full of champagne and carnations, a sight reminiscent of a scene from one of his novels. We three bowled off for London through the night – stopping at Raymond's insistence to drink champagne, the aged chauffeur making a fourth, and wild New Forest ponies wandering up towards the car. Soon Raymond was asleep and Stanford and I talked. Then Raymond, waking as we neared London, said very quietly and soberly: 'I know what you are all doing for me, and I thank you, but the truth is I really *want* to die.' It sounded simple, undramatic, and the natural inspiriting reply seemed suddenly impossible to utter.

Luncheons with each of us, dinners with other friends, or evenings when we battled for hours to lift his depressions continued. His various sagas of his tough-guy exploits or sexual encounters became even more incredible. There was the instant 'affair' with a bejewelled blonde he had met in the lift at the Connaught who was 'just resting' after her umpteenth divorce, and who silently followed him out of the lift to his room on the fourth floor; or there was his heroic, victorious punch-up by which he foiled the attempt by two hoodlums to snatch his wallet; and above all there were stories of rescuing ladies in distress when there was 'no one else around to do it, so I had to'. Some of these tales became part of his life story, congealed (like some of his pet hates amongst acquaintances) into immutability. Though sometimes his hold on reality made him selective about the appropriate audience for certain stories (and his American friends, by some accounts, received an Arabian Nights version of his London life), at other times he could stick to his own account of a situation or even to the person who had actually been a witness of it. His highly dramatized views of our lives (for he treated all the shuttle service friends in a paternalistic manner) were often totally wide of the mark, and it was useless to argue against his strong desire to impose his interpretation. For him we became characters in one of his novels and to introduce our reality into his dream was to arouse his energetic opposition. He often didn't listen or, like a magpie, picked out only the bits which would fit his own picture, which was however always one of genuine solicitude for us and belligerency towards our imagined 'enemies'. He wished to deliver us from the 'hardships' of our lives, and thought of rescuing all of us because 'there was nobody around so I had to', though he could very well see some of the people who were around, but he discounted for rather arbitrary reasons their competence or concern. Nevertheless, his sympathy was genuine and abundant. To Alison he even offered to arrange to have somebody in America bumped off for having ill-treated her – 'It'll cost a thousand bucks!' he said, with a swagger, suggesting that he had only to raise a finger for the Mafia to act, and steadfastly ignoring that she thought this might be going a little *too* far.

Suddenly and rather dramatically he announced he was going to do a drying-out cure at home, and though it was going to be tough he was man enough to take it on. Indeed, in spite of the dramatics, he was. We nursed him on a rota system; I remember Jocelyn coming in one day to take over her turn, looking as fresh as paint, the sad old Raymond in the throes of it, gallantly trying to hurl outrageous witticisms at her, her smiling, droll, and spirited replies, and our most unhappy admiration of his courage and endurance, in which the doctor shared.

He was always immensely preoccupied with thoughts of illness, his own and that of all his friends about whom he became unduly over-anxious, and his letters were full of medical details, his or theirs. I thought it indiscreet of him to tell me such facts about others who might not like me to know them, but it clearly was an obsession of his. He looked for illness in all of us, he wished to return to the life of caring for an invalid, and felt utterly lost without the gentle round of devotion and simple errands he had been used to doing in the tragic previous year, when, he said, he had not been drinking. But by now his desire to care for any invalid could have fulfilment only in fantasy so long as his own health was so precarious. Thus it was, I now think, that of all the shuttle service friends, he wished to be of particular service to me, as the one who could be seen as having been recently ill, though leading the usual hard-working life of concerts, family, and looking after friends, including him. It is now clear that in the friendship which ensued, whilst I was in reality rather energetically organizing the nursing of an ailing Raymond, and Alison teased me about being 'our patrol leader', he was with genuine concern occupied with thoughts of rescuing an invalid; possibly this was satisfying at an unconscious level the search to restore the even tenor of life before his loss.

We were all happy that he had emerged from the drying-out cure relatively free of the big manic swings, our full-time rota was now tapered off, but he was helpless, seeming relieved to be in childlike dependence for a while. We all discussed how to keep him from resuming the solitary and social drinking, for the two were related in his London life, so we decided to suggest a holiday. Alec Murray had throughout this time always answered Raymond's summonses for night nursing, and at first he talked of accompanying Raymond, but a professional job intervened. Since Raymond was concerned for my health, he immediately took up the idea with Stephen and they arranged that I should act as nurse and travel-organizer whilst Raymond recuperated for two weeks at the hotel on Lake Garda where our family always stayed, and where I knew the local doctor well in case of Raymond's needing medical attention, and the friendly proprietor's wife could help if nursing were needed. As a non-drinker and hitherto without experience as nurse to alcoholics, my philosophy was simple: keeping on the move is keeping away from the drink. He was too weak to do any considerable walking, so I arranged local motoring expeditions including ones to Verona and even Venice. He returned to London much stronger, still not drinking, and in a calmer, sunnier state of mind.

He had begun making plans for his return to La Jolla; hitherto an unendurable prospect because of Cissy's lingering presence there. Thereafter he wavered between London and La Jolla. For all that he had been attentively cared for and even at first lionized in London, he often felt socially excluded, for excessive drinking had not improved his popularity as a dinner guest. He complained with some justice of the 'Derrick-Peter-Nigel' routine when at dinner parties a person whom he had never met was discussed, nobody bothering to explain to him. However (I reflected) when that happens either in America or England in my presence, it generally arouses my curiosity about the absent person, he or she sounds more than ordinary, sometimes even exotic, human nature is of inexhaustible interest and I wish to know more. Raymond always wished to know less. It is said that he was suspicious of strangers, and we found that he certainly didn't wish to hear them appreciatively spoken of.

London social life never ceased to amaze him. He met a girl at a dinner-party and had almost automatically described her as showing herself 'open to any proposition', but on his next meeting he found she was 'much less accessible than I thought – she made a very smart and charming appearance and forced me by superior style to act more or less a gentleman ... she simply outmanoeuvred me and all I got out of it was an affectionate embrace in Bedford Square'. Yet all this was play-acting too, since she never had been open to any proposition, nor had he had the intention of making any, and they had entirely engaged in discussions of his various symptoms of ill health, whereupon she had marched him off, much against his wish, to one of the many 'posh doctors'. He saw London social life as 'hypocritical' and never came to realize that London malice is often neither serious nor literal (we like a good joke but don't believe it for a moment, and tacitly assume that nobody else does; the only unforgivable malice is that of passing on unkind remarks). Although he very much enjoyed what he saw as the quick wit of the English, Raymond regarded this as having 'knives for your back' and, for instance, tried seriously to persuade both Stephen and me never to speak again to two of our best friends who had engaged in some harmless joke at our expense.

But would his culture-shock have been so great had he come from New York and had friends of his own mental calibre – rather than from his very cloistered La Jolla life? He wrote to me sadly in 1958: 'If the tax situation permitted, I'd rather come back to England, where at least I have friends.' 'You like America because it is bright and vigorous, I like that part of it too, but with Cissy ill so long I never really had a chance to dig some kindred spirits out of the mob of Philistines and now I'm too tired to want to,' In California, his home with Cissy had been a citadel, almost nobody had been allowed to cross the threshold, so although he was talking of his return there with an air of 'belonging-ness' and he had two devoted intelligent friends who took great care of him, his stay that autumn at a La Jolla hotel was yet another shock. Of the dining-room there he wrote: 'I particularly abhor tables full of middle-aged to elderly females, all dressed to the nines and with bloody awful hats, and all yammering at one another much too loudly in those flat toneless monotonous voices that scratch like fingernails.' He had an almost puritanical hatred for the meaningless hedonism of aimlessly leisured people parading their near-nudity at the swimming pool, and was daunted by the prospect of lonely mealtimes. Small wonder that he seized upon a reason to return to England after a few months. I now don't know how he heard that I was ill, but any illness was always a priority and he surprisingly presented this fact retrospectively to the tax authorities as a rationale for having acted upon his homesickness for England. Late in November he flew back to London.

On this the second period of our seeing him over some weeks, he very soon came to see us, and we were immediately worried by the spectacu-lar deterioration in his state, for he was drinking heavily again. It clearly was to be the same problem as before; alone at the Ritz he would drink, and social life would exacerbate the syndrome. Meanwhile he was startled by the news (which the Spender family took in its stride) that I was to have an operation in mid-December, so when he suggested a trip south to build up my strength, we were both touched by his concern and hopeful that two weeks of rather viligant nursing might improve his own health and morale; though (in retrospect) it was foolish to think that without his doing a preliminary cure it could possibly be effective. The therapeutic success of the previous trip had made us overconfident.

Almost immediately we set off for Tangier, where at first his pleasure in sightseeing and meeting some English friends of ours had a salutary effect. But this time I was no match for alcoholic deviousness; he would frequently be locked incommunicado in his room and make no appearance at mealtimes. Occasionally he appeared more sober, but then he was in a crescendo of anxious misery worse than we had seen in Eaton Square. He spoke almost incessantly of Cissy, but his previous moods of lyricism and resignation had given way to far more complex emotions concerning his whole past life, and he would be submerged in retrospective anger and active despair. To persuade him that all these turbulent feelings about the past were quite natural, that many bereaved people experience them, and to encourage him, as it were, to plough through them, yielded only limited and temporary reassurance, since even when he seemed most affective and heartrending he had the defensive air of one who could not allow himself to acknowledge what he was saying. Although there had been some very enjoyable days, it amazed me afterwards to learn from friends that he had given only a happy account of the trip, particularly of a gloriously sunny day in Chauen, when in fact he was shadowed in silent grumpiness punctuated by descriptions of Cissy's hatred of snow and their sojourns at Bear Lake.

We were all determined that there should be no more of the passive despair of Eaton Square, that none of us would let him slip back into his jettisoning mood. But we were in for a long battle, and it now astonishes me that we didn't then realize the underlying reason for the approaching crisis. His over-dramatic reaction to the operation must have been related to the fact that by coincidence it occured on the anniversary of his wife's death, 12 December. Stephen had quite a time keeping Raymond quiet while I was away at a hospital outside London, for he introduced an element of confusion and havoc where our own family took it calmly and normally. Our family doctor was now looking after Raymond, and finally the long-term effects of his prodigious drinking which he had brought with him from America ended in his being suddenly removed in the night from his hotel to the London Clinic. A two-week cure gave him a fresh lease of life, though Jocelyn said that his very first action, as she helped him out of hospital, was to imbibe the largest Ballantynes she'd ever seen in her life. Nevertheless a post-cure euphoria prevailed.

We didn't ever discover whether our doctor, who was very sensitive to Raymond's need to restore the pride of his Marlowe self-image, had invented an official diagnosis of 'malaria' as a face-saver, but Raymond was delighted that here at last was a doctor who didn't mention his drinking. However, our doctor told us, before bowing out, that there was by now very little hope of reversing the process of deterioration, as did his successor, the local Scottish doctor.

Jocelyn had gone abroad and the others were also away; at the same time Raymond suddenly took a more realistic attitude to his own finances. So we found him a flat near us at Carlton Hill; by this means our travelling could be cut down as we should be mainly the ones looking after him. He found it neither stylish nor comfortable enough, too modest (perforce so, since he was economizing). Its proximity made it easier for us to dash down to shop or cook for him, or to reply to the summonses for help from 'Auntie', his elderly and patient daily housekeeper, sometimes at her wits' end when he was hallucinated and extreme. If he was too ill or drunk to be left alone at night, we used to fetch and care for him at our own house; sometimes Stephen sat up half the night with him when he was insomniac. He wrote appreciatively to Stephen later about his having taken him into our own home when he 'felt lost' and that Stephen and Nick Bentley were the only two men in London who were unfailingly kind to him (I can think of at least two others). The children liked him ('always drunk of course', they said cheerfully), but he was very querulous about them and, though they were very well-behaved, thought that we were, as parents, far too lenient, and that it was unreasonable that he should be expected to answer them during family mealtimes when conversation should be only for grown-ups. 'Any time a five-year-old child is allowed to dominate a dinner table and out-talk everyone else, and I get reproved by you for not answering some unintelligible question the little brat fires at me – any time that happens there's something wrong.' All the same he felt he belonged for he wrote to Stephen early in 1957: 'I rather feel now that the Spender family is my family. And I need the Spender family far more than they need me. Insofar as it is possible I shall always consider myself one of the Spender family.'

Clearly the previous summer had been a false recovery. We had all realized that sporadic euphoria does not show an authentic recovery from grief, but neither did the docility and dependence of his Garda convalescence, which had been, though contented, sometimes almost somnambulist. At that time the true battle had not yet arrived, for though his new friends had provided some continuity of refuge, a new life in a new country was no setting in which he could resolve the ambiguity into which a person is anyway plunged by loss, particularly that loss of every anchor to previously ingrained habits centred on such a long-standing, enclosed ménage. Perhaps the new battle for equilibrium had begun not only because of the approaching emotional storm of the anniversary, but also because his visit to La Jolla had undermined his illusion of 'belongingness', and in his second visit to England he more deeply felt himself to be a refugee rather than being in the interim vacation atmosphere of his first visit.

However, in spite of these overt and more authentic outbursts, delusory elements remained apparent in the over-anxiety and euphoria attached to the outcome of my quite ordinary operation, possibly due to the unconscious purpose of retrieving his own lost past, for the fact that one of his new protective companions had *survived* may have given him an unconscious feeling of reprieve from the prospect of the continued inner turmoil of grief which was the dynamic underlying preoccupation. He then published an article about Cissy's death which seemed to be both a renewed attempt to enact a tender farewell gesture, and an act of covert reparation for the violent feelings about the past which had so recently engulfed him, and for which he had shown signs of feeling guilt.

So the overriding reason for bad times at Carlton Hill was drink, I believe, to drown the fiercely conflicting images of his past life; and any other reason he projected to certain selected friends of his was a self-deception similar to reasons he had invented in earlier crises to explain, for instance, the abrupt end of his oil-tycoon career. But there were also good times when his wit and originality sprang into life again and he would improvise more serial tales of adventure. An expedition to Cambridge to meet Frances Cornford amused him. Having asked him what was his favourite expression in the American vernacular, she was visibly startled when he replied vigorously: 'Aw, turn blue.'

Some of us spent a number of peaceful afternoons helping Raymond sort the many letters of sympathy and fellow feeling from bereaved readers of the *Daily Express* to whom his rather Victorian and elegiac picture of mourning farewell had brought comfort. He also invited some of these correspondents to tea, and would afterwards retail their stories with a great deal of feeling. But there were also more suicide attempts, after which he would seem shamefaced and almost contented, and a very strange hallucinatory incident which frightened 'Auntie' into calling us for help, when he appeared to be re-enacting his original La Jolla suicide attempt. It is curious that in *The Long Goodbye* his attitude to suicide is far tougher than that which we all felt towards these suicidal crises. There Philip Marlowe (his good self) says to Roger Wade (his bad self): 'Nobody can stop you from killing youself if you really want to. I realize that. So do you.'

By now his cries for help had become intensified, as I was the last surviving shuttle-service friend upon whom he totally depended, though he made lengthy nocturnal telephone calls to Jocelyn in Paris, who always raised his spirits. My own anxious concern that his survival seemed so problematical, and my distress about his evident loneliness became the target for his endeavour to project his illusory views about the form he thought my life should take. His great need for nursing companionship would lead him blindly to ignore my devotion to my family and to music, and he would sometimes demand more time than I could spare from work and family, and test out my staying power as a friend by expressing views reflecting a divorce from reality which was beyond the powers of compassion to resolve. These weeks became the peak of his battle towards grasping the reality of Cissy's death and the unreality of his 'play-acting' attempts (as he later described them) to substitute a fantasized 'romantic whirl of enjoyment of London life' for the natural process of allowing his complex grief to work itself out without either projection or denial. He later expressed his own sense of the truth of this explanation of his Carlton Hill crisis to Stephen, when giving him a far too generous account of my role at that time and an equally generous expression of reciprocal solicitude for my health. 'I am willing to stake anything to get Natasha well. After all she alone gave me the impetus and motive for curing myself' (not true – we *all* did something towards it). 'I shouldn't have cared to do it for myself. She alone had the infinite patience to see me go through crisis after crisis without once coming even near to giving me up as a bad job. The doctors could cure me temporarily, but they could not give me back a soul. Only Natasha could be steadfast enough to do that!' Actually I have since wondered sometimes whether patience *was* the most salutary help to offer, for sometimes I felt forced to leave the room, if for instance he expressed hostility to children (there argument was not possible, for his feeling of that deprivation in his past life was the saddest part of his illness). I had so often admired Jocelyn's more cheerfully forthright way of dealing with crises at Eaton Square, for if he hectored, she could hector back, gracefully turning his contentiousness into a jocular vein in which it became too silly for him to persist. However, at Carlton Hill his fight for equilibrium was on a much more profound level. Arguments of the form 'I know I'm bad and it's tiny steps for tiny feet, but your beliefs commit you to *having* to help me,' invoked when he was desperate, were tiring; though sometimes, like Jocelyn, I could turn him towards the jokes he could seldom resist.

Yet one might say there was a clash of codes. Raymond thought the belief I had in *caritas* and prayer either mysterious or an abdication of intellectual control; and I thought his cynical views and fundamental distrust of everyone's goodwill too pessimistic about human nature. The battle against his slow suicide resolved itself into persuading him that with all their faults it's worth living amongst other people – quite a number of them, *all* his friends to start with. But this attitude had never before prevailed in his life; despite mixed feelings, his dominant attitude had always been the total commitment to Cissy, and protective intolerance towards others. Though still fundamentally absorbed by Cissy, he looked forward to finding a similar protective isolation through another person, where he might exclude the rest of the 'dangerous' outside world and continue his creative work within such a haven. Except for what he himself later described as an earlier 'brief moment of infatuation', he had always realized that this had never been a prospect with me nor any other member of the shuttle-service. As soon as he returned to America in May 1956 he continued a search with a succession of people in La Jolla to re-establish a *cloître à deux* – an unrealistic search. But all that can be said of the victory which we in the shuttle-service, and later I in particular, had helped him achieve was as he later wrote in March 1957: 'You made me realize that whatever one has suffered, to resign from life is just silly.'

His loneliness at the end of his life was painful to see and revives equally distressing memories of that of Auden at the end of his life.

Although Auden was a far closer and more long-standing friend, and we had beliefs in common, sitting over luncheon at Carlton Hill was quite like sitting over tea in our kitchen in Loudoun Road with Auden, discussing 'LIFE'. Though their achievements were of a totally different order, in history they were not unlike; both devoted to memories of 'saintly' mothers and both always searching to be mothered, both concerned with the discipline aspect of writing and justly proud of their craftsmanship, both in old age nervy and demanding, both childless, both drinking, and both craving only companionship and a gentle round of domestic chores – nothing more. But where Raymond in work and life was sentimental, a fantasist and self-deluding (his drinking had a long life history), even self-pitying, Auden was absolutely non-fantasist, controlled and stoic, his daily litany being a counting of his blessings. In Raymond it is possible that childlessness explained his skirmishes against both Christianity and psychoanalysis, for both creeds recognize the primacy, vulnerability and sacredness of childhood. Auden's Christianity originated in his relationship to a loving mother; his compassion was easily accommodated in both creeds, Raymond on occasions found it hard to keep in touch with his. Raymond was proud to think of himself as a 'passionate moralist', which sounds comparatively merciless towards himself and others; Auden believed benevolently in redemption and forgiveness, and was a 'compassionate moralist'. Perhaps Raymond's anti-Christianity (although here is a contradiction, for later he claimed to be Christian) was part of his dominant modes of defence, projection and denial in fantasy, since he so valued 'pride' and 'toughness' that he would not have cared to classify them amongst the Seven Deadly Sins. Nevertheless he could sometimes be disarmingly modest.

Towards psychoanalysis Raymond always maintained a wary if not belligerent attitude. At one of those first luncheons at the Connaught when I remarked that our neuroses mostly originate in childhood, he replied with scornful, teasing gusto: 'Oh, I don't know – I pick mine up as I go along.' (It is true that one of his recurrent ambivalences between over-confidence and anxiety, generosity and apprehension – his attitude to money – probably had at least been traumatically re-activated by a shock he sustained in early married life when he lost an important job and his financial security because of drinking.) He was also defiantly proud to tell of having repudiated the help of the 'trick-cyclist' at the clinic after his first suicide attempt by saying: 'Doctor, if you'll be perfectly frank with me ... I may be able to help you.' Certainly Raymond

A moustachioed Marlowe (George
Montgomery) gets it in the neck in *The
Brasher Doubloon*, 1947.

ABOVE: Marlowe (Robert Mitchum) talks things over with LA cops (*left*, Harry Dean Stanton and *centre*, John Ireland as Lieutenant Nulty) in *Farewell, My Lovely*, 1975.

BELOW: Marlowe accompanies Moose Malloy (Jack O'Halloran) aboard Brunette's gambling ship.

Dick Powell in *Murder, My Sweet* ('Farewell, My Lovely'), 1944.

Humphrey Bogart in *The Big Sleep*, 1946.

TOP: Robert Montgomery in *The Lady in the Lake*, 1946.
BOTTOM: George Montgomery in *The Brasher Doubloon* ('The High Window'), 1947.

TOP: Van Heflin, the American radio Marlowe, 1947.
BOTTOM: Gerald Mohr, who played Marlowe on the radio from 1947–50.

TOP: Philip Carey in the TV series *Philip Marlowe*, 1959.

BOTTOM: James Garner in *Marlowe* ('The Little Sister'), 1969.

TOP: Elliott Gould in *The Long Goodbye*, 1972.

BOTTOM: Robert Mitchum in *Farewell, My Lovely*, 1975.

TOP: Claire Trevor as Velma/Mrs Grayle
(*Murder, My Sweet*).
BOTTOM: Lauren Bacall as Vivien Reagan
(*The Big Sleep*).

TOP: Martha Vickers as Carmen Sternwood
(*The Big Sleep*).
BOTTOM: Audrey Totter as Adrienne
Fromsett (*The Lady in the Lake*).

TOP: Nancy Guild as Merle Davis (*The Brasher Doubloon*).
BOTTOM: Gayle Hunnicutt as Mavis Weld (*Marlowe*).

TOP: Nina Van Pallandt as Eileen Wade (*The Long Goodbye*).
BOTTOM: Charlotte Rampling as Velma/Mrs Grayle (*Farewell, My Lovely*).

Veronica Lake as Joyce Harwood (*The Blue Dahlia*).

Barbara Stanwyck as Phyllis Dietrichson (*Double Indemnity*).

was a character of opposites, and hated his own Roger Wade 'bad self' with its bitterness. Nevertheless, he was right to express his opinion of my lack of realism later to Stephen by saying that I was 'in love with complete goodness'. 'I side with you,' he wrote to Stephen, 'the devil is part of the being of every creative person.'

When Raymond left England again after Easter (during which once more we had been away with the children) he went to stay with friends in Old Chatham, New York, before, finally, the long months of continuous drinking caught up with him and, dangerously ill, he was suddenly rushed into a New York hospital. From there he wrote shakily by hand, thanking me for a 'wonderful' letter and saying that he had had a curious mystical experience after five days' illness, having woken with a curious lightness of the heart, as though the 'long nightmare' was over at last, and he had been 'absolved'. It is true that he never again talked at length of the 'long nightmare', though at Palm Springs we all saw unacknowledged reverberations of it.

The end of Carlton Hill had marked the end of the shuttle-service as such, though we all remained friends; his will to live had survived the long-drawn-out crises which culminated in the New York hospital. The suicide threats were over, but I don't believe we had any of us had the faintest effect on his drinking except for short periods of vigilant care.

The last of the three periods during which I saw Raymond consecutively lasted a few weeks at the end of my American concert tour in December 1956. He had telephoned sounding positively jaunty, energetic and (I thought probably) well, and was longing to discuss all his Californian life plans including matrimonial ones, for he had spent five months or so seeing a great deal of someone he had planned to marry, but at the last moment they had decided not to go ahead; he was still at times hovering, yet already thinking of other possibilities in La Jolla and said that he needed my advice. He was keen on 'desert air' and with his usual solicitude invited me for a two-week rest cure to Arizona (for I had been ordered off work for a few weeks) after which I should go on to Los Angeles and resume my concert tour. I had clearly not been a good Angeles and resume my concert tour. I had clearly not been a good judge of his state by telephone, for when he met me by car at Phoenix airport on 6 December he was again very jangled and drunk and drove the car alarmingly, driving first of all straight into a fence, and then weaving across and even off the road, so that it was a miracle that we arrived in Chandler, Arizona without disaster. Never in my life have I been so near to jumping out of a moving vehicle.

It took a nightmare vigil of some days to sober him up, after which time with the well-known self-deception of the alcoholic he wrote an affectionate letter to 'My Very Dear Stephen' saying how *well* he was. 'I do not get drunk, obstreperous and think or say the unkind and often bitter things I used to say with what I now regard as frightful arrogance and lack of Christian charity.' Indeed, as soon as he *had* recovered from the very bad start and we had set out on the tour ranging from Tucson through almost every canyon and desert, I saw that in forward-looking realism his spirit *was* transformed since his last stay in London, and the usual 'travel therapy' restored his health. He was his amused and amusing paternalistic self throughout the trip and, as he described it, had become self-reliant. He talked of finishing a novel (the first talk of work since we had known him, for Helga Greene had some time previously in 1956 become his agent and was encouraging him with plans). The upset about the marriage disappointment had calmed down; though he was intending marriage somehow in the future, talked of the possibility of a Texan divorcée, or of another very nice ex-wife of a friend, or simply hoped with Micawberish optimism, someone would turn up. He would live in La Jolla, 'but emphatically not alone' he said with cheerful self-confidence. I left him happily planning a longer stay in Palm Springs (after we had given Stephen and the family a pre-Christmas telephone call) and myself went off on a round of visits ending up in Los Angeles on New Year's Eve with my friends Professor and Dr Edward Hooker; where I started practising again for later concerts.

Evelyn Hooker is a psychologist, and as we were very close friends, I asked her prognosis about the whole story of Raymond's fight for recovery, so that when we heard he was to arrive in Los Angeles on 6 January she was sympathetically looking forward to meeting 'the impatient patient', as he sometimes called himself. I was now rather keen to get back to work, to stay on with the Hookers practising the piano, but meanwhile he had with great solicitude written to Stephen urging him to use his influence to persuade me to stay in the desert until I was 'really well' for he was, as always, very concerned for my health and pianistic career, and eager to do something in return for the earlier help he felt I had been to him. He had always regarded his role as that of patron, though his ideas of a musical career were unrealistically 'Hollywood'. He was very impressed that I played concertos at the

Royal Albert Hall or on television but curiously enough he never heard a concert of mine.

When Raymond arrived, the Hookers were both so alarmed by his once more being in a totally unsteady and distraught state that they tried to dissuade me from looking after him, since I was myself still in need of rest, and their opinion was that he very much needed the sort of psychiatric care which I was not equipped to give. However, I had by now already promised a short visit and feared to disappoint him in his present precarious state. Christopher Isherwood was an admirer of Raymond's powerful evocation of Los Angeles in all his novels so Raymond took us for lunch and a perilously erratic drive round *his* Los Angeles, taking both hands off the wheel to gesture grandly: 'That's where Bugsie Siegel was SHOT!' and recapturing scenes which he had used in his novels.

That evening Gerald Heard and Raymond came to dine at the Hookers, and as always I found Gerald's gentle, erudite, mandarin brilliance a peaceful delight. Topics ranged widely: mescalin, Chinese jades, the piano music of Schubert, Tolkien, and the private life of Dr Swift, all of which Raymond found very boring, and Evelyn and Edward Hooker's cheerful attentive efforts to engage Raymond in conversation were of little avail. Christopher Isherwood and Don Bachardy joined us after dinner, but even Christopher's appreciative account of our afternoon drive failed to mollify Raymond's feeling of exclusion ('Derrick-Peter-Nigel') so often engendered when subjects unfamiliar to him were discussed.

I didn't ever discover whether his upset state was due to some more recent drama or development in his La Jolla life-plans during the previous two weeks, or whether it was simply a result of solitary drinking. The following afternoon he arrived at the Hookers' looking very burly in a red lumber-man's cap and we drove to Palm Springs through sheets of driving rain. There for five days a quiet regime of work (the first time I had ever seen signs of daily work on a novel), swimming, more vitamin pills, less drink and daily visits to the movies somewhat restored his well being, when on the sixth day news was brought to us of the sudden death of Edward Hooker. I wished to return directly to be with Evelyn, but Raymond was suddenly so distraught that she and I decided that I would return only after three days for the funeral service. I tried to conceal from Raymond my sadness, but his continued irritability led me to consult Christopher by telephone, and we arranged that at the weekend we should all return to Palm Springs together so that Evelyn could get away from her house and be with friends, and Raymond also would have company. Inevitably he was to be left alone for some days whilst I stayed with Evelyn, with whom I drove back from Los Angeles to Palm Springs, Christopher and Don Bachardy arriving the following morning.

Raymond, delighted to see us all again, seemed strangely jolly, then grumpy, once again dissociated from reality but always animated and contented in Christopher's company, and responsive to Christopher's off-beat humour. Evelyn was superb, joining in when she could, disappearing to rest when she felt unequal to it. Raymond was by turns querulous then high-spirited and seemingly quite unaware of the undertow of deep concern and admiration the rest of us had for Evelyn.

One afternoon we all discussed religion. Christopher talked of meditation, and I was surprised that Raymond, generally so opaque to all such ideas, seemed genuinely absorbed by it. He returned to the subject of meditation again and again but reiterated his adamant belief that 'Cissy is gone for ever', and said he could only relate that fact to the futility of other people's prayers which he saw as fundamentally no more than 'asking for things' which, he said, he would be too proud to do. That suggests that there was always only one thing he would wish to ask for – and that he knew to be irrational. We did not ever manage to convince him that one need have no concern with (nor belief in) personal survival nor even with the nature or existence of God, yet still be disposed to practise meditation. To me it seemed analogous to the concentration enjoyed by the interpretive musician, but I did not ever detect in Raymond that sort of aesthetic orientation which might have given meaning to the analogy.

It was only when we all talked of leaving for Los Angeles that he became suddenly irate, monopolizing attention and totally unsympathetic to Evelyn's needs and my desire to be with her in *her* bereavement. We realized that this proximity to a sudden death had put Raymond back into his own traumatic time of the same season two years previously, and he was making himself quite ill with anxiety. So we all gave up the idea of my immediate return, the heroic Evelyn insisting that I stayed on an extra four days until I felt reasonably sure he had recovered his poise. I later learned that he had minded my spending even the two last days of my California time with Evelyn before my departure. This became one of those incidents to be congealed in his mind in immutable grievance; I had failed him as a good friend. But I had seen no sign of vexation about it at the time, nor any disturbances other than the extremity evoked by Edward's death.

However, he continued to telephone Evelyn, to read her various bits of nonsense he had written in the hope of cheering her up and wrote later to me: 'I think I really have a friend there, a very real friend.' Throughout February he sounded cheerful (though beset with laryngitis and dermatological ills described at length) but the great news was that already he had a 'sweet new Australian secretary' and was being well looked after, to our great relief. Her enterprising spirit soon pervaded his life, and he praised her honesty, as he did mine. He was very soon immensely involved with helping her get a divorce, but also seemed briefly concerned with the pursuit of a lady he had spoken of when in Arizona (not, however, thought so intelligent as his secretary), so his La Jolla matrimonial plans seemed already well under way. He wrote and telephoned us often about the Australian family drama which increasingly absorbed him; he was clearly very fond of them; here at last was a family to which he could become the father (or rather the stepfather he himself had never had); he seemed firmly established in a new life, though desirous of bringing his family to London, rather than facing with them a new (for him) country, Australia. So I was happily convinced (possibly again being too sanguine) that in his new life-plans, bereavement plus the desire for a childless *cloître à deux*, which he had sought with his previous American fiancée, were finally over for good.

However, he was in a protracted and annoying battle over tax liability and residential status, so although homesick for England his enforced absence coloured his attitude, and his tone became changeable (as it often did when he was drinking more). It was critical of English life, fickle about some English friends he had hitherto been fond of. Though I wrote and he telephoned fairly often, generally about his secretary's divorce proceedings, I was not so assiduous a correspondent as he. He protested about this (sometimes with justice), though there was a continual discussion of his plans and hopes of our meeting him and his new family after the summer holidays. After a dearth of letters from me, in June I received a sad letter from La Jolla in which he wrote: 'I don't care about your neglect of me at all – only that you should understand if you want to, how I feel. I was rather stupid all along. You were so kind and tender to me in my troubles that I believed it was to me, not merely to someone in trouble. I now know that I was wrong, that you would have done the same for anyone in deep trouble.' Yet in spite of its valedictory tone and the projection upon me of a fantasy, to account for his feeling distanced from us not only geographically but also by his new commitments, our friendship and the flow of his letters went on without a break.

After a week or so the erratic post had delivered three of my letters and my silence was forgiven, suggesting that his over-reaction to it had been another of those dramatic inabilities to 'play any part quite straight'. A gloriously funny letter arrived saying that he had been trying to think all day of things not to forgive me for and had finally remembered an antique grievance: 'When you were going to have that last party for me I made the overripe gesture of trying to contribute six bottles of champagne; whereupon in your most stuffy voice: "I'd much rather not. When the Spenders entertain, they like to provide their own refreshments." And then: "I think I'll give you a Talbot," in a voice that suggested you were going to give me the lower half of the Queen of Sheba. So I dutifully cancelled the order for the champagne, feeling rather whipped ... Now I'm not scolding you any more.'

I hope and assume that I managed to persuade him that, although one would do the same for anyone in trouble, I certainly did not lose the affectionate concern which, although he had for some time no longer needed us in the way he had at first, our whole family retained for him. These friendships with despairing people start out in an emergency, as if by chance one were the only bystander at a street accident and gave what first aid one could. The traumatic despair of its origins always remains, however submerged, the fundamental ground-bass theme of the friendship. When resolution of the baffling ambiguity of grief moves towards a relinquishing of the dependence of crisis time and towards a more realistic independence, then the process can be experienced as a painful deferred echo of the original loss and it can evoke similar reactions, even when a new life is already embarked upon. Just as I have seen many times the brief, initial, positive transference with bereaved or divorced women friends who have for a time been in need of great support, so also the deferred echo has often appeared when a more equable balance of friendship is established.

In August Raymond's secretary wrote that I was not to be surprised if his letters were not clearheaded: he was in hospital after another bad drinking bout and had three special nurses round the clock whom he did not need, for he had made an excellent recovery; but they kept him occupied and he was enjoying the constant attention! But he soon wrote a number of letters describing all symptoms and diagnoses (of course, none of them faintly related to drink) yet already, except for a fractured wrist, seemingly quite recovered in every way. During that autumn, though as usual beset by various ailments, he sounded more happily engrossed in work. He finished *Playback* and enjoyed his stay in Palm Springs when Helga Greene visited him. She had by this time become a closer friend. Their community of professional interests began to flourish as the bereavement receded into the past, and she did immensely well for him.

It was not until the following February (1958) that he returned to London and took a flat in Chelsea, where he stayed until August. This time he was looked after by a male nurse (which he had needed and should have had in Carlton Hill, but we had had no authority to arrange it) and also until she left for a trip to Australia by his Australian secretary. He seemed proud of his new family and that the children trusted and liked him. His life was admirably organized by Helga Greene who had fostered and encouraged the work on finishing *Playback*. We saw him at meals occasionally through that summer, and I found him in quieter good humour and, I hoped, happier than on previous visits. He had aged; there was less sparkle, less vehemence, little contention and more gentle geniality.

I remember Stephen and I having invited him to lunch at the Cate Royal grill to meet a talented young writer, Frank Norman, whose account of prison life Stephen had first published in *Encounter* and whose first book needed a resonant introduction. Raymond wrote it, the only work he completed in 1958. Though older and more frail, Raymond still retained his rather swashbuckling manner. Frank had lived nearly all his life in orphanages, Borstals or prison, and Raymond became very excited at meeting (as he over-dramatized it to himself) this 'hardened criminal', which Frank was very far from ever having been. Raymond hectored Frank quite considerably, with a seeming vicarious desire for an atmosphere of violence, whereas Frank was quiet, cheerful, and I thought admirably dignified under this onslaught. When Raymond said for about the sixth time, with a theatrical tough-guy heave of the shoulders: '*You'll* never go straight,' Frank replied quietly: 'I hope, if I have to, that I'll have the guts to earn my living mending roads.'

Raymond also came to stay in the Oxfordshire cottage where we were living for that summer, in one of the most beautiful large gardens in England, but London seemed to have become his centre of gravity at last and enjoyment of the Cotswold quiet, if he had any at all, was transient. He was amiable, unusually tolerant, and bored. During that autumn his letters were cheerfully nostalgic, particularly about Venice where Stephen and I had stayed. In the New Year the Spender family moved to San Francisco.

In March 1959 we were planning to drive down from Berkeley to visit him in La Jolla but at the last moment he telephoned to say he was suddenly leaving for England with Helga who, we were glad to hear, had just accepted his proposal of marriage. It was a gossipy, affectionate telephone call: and I was happy (amid later sorrow) to have had that half-hour of cloudless friendship, for less than three weeks later he was dead.

The Illusion of The Real

JACQUES BARZUN

By a complicated series of chances, it began to strike some writers in the late 1920s and 1930s that crime fiction might possibly be written so as to qualify as 'literature'. One favouring fact was that actual crime seemed no longer beyond the pale but central to social existence – the disaster of the Prohibition Law had helped make the point. Another encouragement came from the delight with which readers of the Naturalistic novel swallowed the sordid and learned the language of thieves. Finally, trade practices suggested that any prose fiction of standard length could be palmed off as a novel, although it might in fact be a tale, that is to say a narrative answering quite different requirements from the novel proper, which has social obligations and must pay its debt to psychology.

The upshot was that Dashiell Hammett and after him James M. Cain and Raymond Chandler undertook to 'raise' the detective genre into the circle of respectable reading matter – as if the best minds had not already discovered the pleasures of crime fiction taken on its own merits. The justification for this self-conscious and self-righteous effort to elevate a genre was the syllogism that literature deals with reality, that the sign of reality is horror and squalor, and hence that a tale impregnated with these flavours would – other things equal – be literature.

We may be grateful that from these fallacies so much good work has come. But there is no warrant for the commonly held belief that the tough detective tale yields greater truth than the gentler classical form and marks a forward step toward 'the real novel'. The 'soft' genteel story, in which the corpse is found in a library by the butler, may be a period piece, but is in itself neither truer nor falser than the story set in the back alleys of Glasgow or Los Angeles. Butlers may be an anachronism, but so are bootleggers – and private libraries are still more numerous than private eyes. Nor is habitual vulgarity of speech 'more real' than civil talk among educated people.

On these points the literary mind has been influenced and – as it seems to me – perverted, by Raymond Chandler's famous essay. His definition of 'The Simple Art of Murder' was taken as the burial service read over the corpse of the classical tale, and his words were reprinted over and over again.

To make his case, Chandler took A.A. Milne's *Red House Mystery* and showed how it violated the plausible in action, motive, police routine, and the expression of human feeling. Some of his points were unquestionably telling, both about Milne's work and about the tradition its critic made it stand for. But Chandler started from an untenable premise in his first sentence: 'Fiction in any form has always tended to be realistic.' And he never bothered to analyse what he meant by realism. So he never saw the other side of the coin, which shows, not that the classical mode is more real than Chandler admits, but that realness is irrelevant.

This must be so, since the tough mode, including Chandler's own admirable work, is open to the same objections as the other. Consider the tough formula: a private detective, usually low in funds and repute, undertakes single-handed and often without fee the vindication of some unfortunate person – a man or woman with no other friends. The attempt pits the hero against a ruthless crime syndicate or against the whole corrupt government of the town, or both. During his search for evidence, he is threatened, slugged, drugged, shot at, kidnapped, tortured, but never downed for very long. In many of the variants of the genre, he drinks quantities of whiskey neat and proves equally ready for fighting and fornication. None of this affects his work; he is guaranteed indestructible. Others' bullets pass him by; his own – especially in the final scene of carnage – always find their mark. And despite the gruelling physical pace, he finds the time and the wit, without the aid of discussion or note-taking, to figure out the discrepancies that reveal the culprit and his motive.

Now if in comparing the tender and the tough conventions one is looking for 'real life' in the verifiable sense, one must conclude that although the first kind of story will not bear sceptical examination, the second is – as Shakespeare says apropos of two liars – 'an even more wonderful song than the other'. Nor is this all that Raymond Chandler's essay brings to mind. The tender school aims at producing a denouement having the force of necessity, as in Greek tragedy. All the facts (clues, words, motives) must converge to give the mystery one solution and one only. That by itself is a good reason for making the crime occur in a law-abiding circle, where the habits of the *dramatis personae* are by hypothesis regular and reasonable. In such a setting the violence of murder is the more striking, and stronger also the desire to manacle the offender. Murder among thugs and drug addicts is hardly unexpected, and the feeling that in this milieu anything can happen does not increase but rather lessens the interest. Hence the artistic need for the tough writer to involve some innocent, whose ways *are* peaceable, and to put steadily in peril the detective-defender of that lump of virtue. In short, in murder à la Chandler, murder is not enough to keep us going – and neither is detection, since it is never a feature of the foreground.

Chandler as artist is so aware of these lacks that he reinforces the damsel-in-distress motive with what is nothing less than a political motive. He makes it clear in his essay that the hero of the new and improved genre is fighting society. Except for the favoured victim, he alone is pure in heart, a C-green incorruptible. The rich are all crooked or 'phonies', and cowards in the end. Since the police, the mayor, the whole Establishment are soon shown as a conspiracy to pervert justice and kill off troublemakers, we naturally share the detective's smothered indignation and are powerfully driven, like him, to see the right vindicated.

The tough story was born in the Thirties and shows the Marxist colouring of its birth years. It follows that in Chandler's essay the critique of the classical formula seems to spring not solely from a mistaken demand for realism, but also from a hostility to the solvent way of life. That the well-to-do could be honest, 'genuine', and lovable apparently was not 'realistic' either. And obviously the reader was to feel morally uplifted by the solemn conclusion describing the true hero-detective ('The Simple Art of Murder'):

> He must be a complete man and a common man and yet an unusual man ... He must be the best man in his world and a good enough man for any world ... He is a relatively poor man, or he would not be a detective at all. ... He will take no man's money dishonestly and no man's insolence without a due and dispassionate revenge. He is a lonely man and his pride is that you will treat him as a proud man or be very sorry you ever saw him. The story is this man's adventure in search of a hidden truth ... If there were enough like him, the world would be a very safe place to live in, without becoming too dull to be worth living in.

Who's the sentimental tale-spinner now? After thirty years it makes no difference to our enjoyment of the great sagas by Chandler, Ross Macdonald, and others that the eternal Robin Hood should have got mixed up with Marx's angry young men and Tennyson's Galahad, and wound up in self-contradiction. What was and remains comic is that Chandler should have chosen for his California hero the name Philip Marlowe, which from first name to final *e* connotes Englishness, Elegance, and Establishment.

What has happened since Chandler and his essay is that his imitators and amplifiers have used his pseudo-realism to convey the mood or message of their particular decade. Sometimes this burden is no more than a set of slogans and catchphrases. But it is of interest to the cultural historian that every few years the attitude and grievances rather unnecessarily expressed by the heroes of crime fiction alter noticeably, and in so doing follow the prevailing wind of social thought, the latest view that Western man holds about the world.

A study of the best writers would even show that the emotions now acted out in nihilistic vandalism and violence were first voiced by the sympathetic heroes in such tales, and that the shift of moral preference from law-abiding to criminal behaviour was first popularized through these new-style Byronic rebels and self-haters. In this respect, of course, the tough tale of crime and detection can lay claim to being a criticism of life, even if it is only an echo of that criticism. But then the classic detective genre, which is not tough, not realism, not a facsimile of the novel, remains as the useful, pleasurable, and still flourishing account of a vanishing type of existence, ethical, civilized, and in the best sense literary.

Friend and Mentor

FRANK NORMAN

When Stephen Spender told me that Raymond Chandler had read the ten thousand word extracts of my prison memoir *Bang to Rights* in the May 1958 edition of *Encounter* and wanted to meet me, I had no idea who he was, nor was I much the wiser after Spender explained. Never having been any good at remembering anyone's name until I've actually met them, and sometimes not even then, I went around for several days telling people that I had a lunch date with Raymond Chandley the detective story writer at the Café Royal next Friday.

The trouble with mentors is that you can rarely choose your own. They choose you and you almost always end up being a terrible disappointment to them. Ray was my friend and mentor for the last ten months of his life – too short a period for me to become a disappointment to him, thank God.

The fifty quid that the highbrow monthly paid me for the extracts from the rough and ready manuscript of *Bang to Rights* had, by the morning of our celebrated meeting, dwindled to a few shillings – enough for the tube fare from Hampstead to the West End and a packet of fags. My dark pinstripe suit had seen better days – it was the same one that I'd been wearing in the dock at the County of London Sessions on the 26 April 1955 when the judge gave me three years for bouncing dud cheques. It had lain in a brown paper parcel in my property at Camp Hill Prison on the Isle of Wight for two years – the moth had chewed holes in the crotch and the back of the jacket was as shiny as a guardsman's boots.

Spender and I were already seated at a table when Ray arrived – four sheets to the wind he reeled across the room in our direction, leaving jogged elbows and soup-splattered shirt fronts in his wake. He was an elderly man with dishevelled grey hair and hornrimmed spectacles, nattily turned out in an expensively cut navy blue suit, crumpled polka dot bow tie and white gloves and he was carrying a silver knobbed cane. He wore gloves even at meal times to hide a skin ailment.

I gather from Frank MacShane's mention of our first meeting in his biography of Chandler that Ray '... was excited by the prospect of meeting what he imagined was a hardened criminal'. Which might account for the first words he spoke to me when Spender introduced us.

'Howdy, scarface,' he grinned and offered his hand.

I hope I returned his smile, but not being too ready with smiles in those days, I may not have.

He'd over-trained for lunch and was pretty drunk. But this, I soon learned, was his usual condition any time after ten or eleven in the morning. I don't recall ever seeing him completely sober. He ordered a large whisky and a plate of spaghetti which he spilled into his lap as soon as it arrived. I like people who do things like that. I warmed to him instantly and felt sure that we were going to be friends.

After lunch I strolled the short distance with him to the Ritz Hotel, where he'd taken a suite and as we parted company he asked me quietly if I would let him read the rest of the manuscript of *Bang to Rights*. I brought it around to him the following day and a week later I was having lunch with him again, this time in his suite at the Ritz.

Over a couple of mammoth tumblers of whisky, soda and ice (Ray poured the biggest drinks in the world), he told me that he'd enjoyed the rest of the manuscript as much as the *Encounter* extracts and offered to write a foreword to the book when I found a publisher for it. Then the waiter came in and took down our orders for lunch. I asked for steak, peas and chips. The steak and peas arrived in the fullness of time but not the chips and when it became obvious that the waiter had forgotten about them I politely jogged his memory.

'You didn't order French fried potatoes, sir,' he sniffed.

'Yes I did.'

'You are mistaken, sir.'

'No I'm not,' I snarled. 'I ordered chips and you wrote chips down on your pad.'

'If that was the case, sir,' he came back at me belligerently, 'they would be here.'

'Would it be all right,' I enquired quite hotly, 'if I ordered some chips now?'

'Yes, sir,' he grunted and departed in a huff.

'Well done, Frank,' cried Ray. 'I don't think I'd ever get up the nerve to put a Ritz waiter in his place.'

His praise baffled me – I'd not realized that one did not argue with waiters in polite society and had merely followed my natural instincts.

A week or two before I met Ray he'd been on a *Sunday Times* assignment in Rome where, after considerable difficulty, he'd managed to secure an interview with Lucky Luciano the Mafia racketeer recently deported from America. How he could have been 'excited' to meet a down-at-heel, small-time yobo like me after keeping that kind of company remains a mystery. He showed me the article he'd written about

Luciano and was extremely resentful that the editor of the *Sunday Times* had declined to publish it on the grounds that it was libellous.

Encounter, in those days, was published by Secker & Warburg and financed, it was revealed years later, by the CIA – it's a great pity that we've been deprived of the wisecrack that Ray would undoubtedly have made about that. Secker took *Bang to Rights* shortly after the extracts appeared and Ray duly contributed his promised foreword: 'There is no damned literary nonsense about his writing.' he wrote, 'Frank Norman writes swiftly and closely about things ... An observation so sharp should not be lost to the world. We need it. He has it.' It was the only time in his life that he helped a young writer in that particular way. It was a lot to live up to.

We saw quite a lot of each other that summer. He moved out of the Ritz and went to live in a rented ground floor flat at 8, Swan Walk, on the Chelsea Embankment. In August he published *Playback*, the last of the Philip Marlowe stories. Soon after it came out he invited me around to lunch at Swan Walk. He was moderately sober when I arrived and was being looked after by a male nurse named Don. Ray welcomed me in his usual warm-hearted way and Don grilled a couple of chops for us.

'What've you been doing?' asked Ray.

I told him that I'd just completed the first draft of a three-act play entitled *Fings Ain't Wot They Used T'Be*. But quickly added that I didn't know the first thing about writing plays and had just typed out forty-eight foolscap pages of dialogue off the top of my head and it'd taken me a week.

'Don't worry about that,' he said. 'When I first started writing novels I couldn't get anyone's hat off their head.'

After lunch we talked and swigged whisky for an hour or two, then Ray phoned a car-hire firm that he often used and asked for a limousine to be sent around to take me home. Before I left he gave me an inscribed copy of *Playback*: 'For Frank Norman a recent but by now a close friend. Raymond Chandler. London, August 1958,' he scrawled.

Later in the afternoon he called me up on the pay-phone in the hall of the house in Hampstead where I had a bedsitter.

'Did you tip the chauffeur?' he asked.

'Yes.'

'How much?'

'Half a crown.'

'Well, he shouldn't have taken it,' he replied angrily. 'I told him not to take any money from you.'

I accompanied Ray and his literary agent and friend, Helga Greene, to the theatre one evening to see a play by Donald Ogden Stewart entitled *The Kidders*. Ray nodded off the moment the curtain rose – the end of the first act was marked by a pistol shot on stage and he awoke with a start and said: 'One gun shot doesn't make a play.'

In mid-August he flew home to La Jolla, California and I did not see him again. But I did get three letters from him, the first is dated 9 September 1958 and reads, in part: 'I hope things are going well with you. If you are in financial trouble, please get in touch with me or Helga, because neither of us wishes lack of money to cause you to fall into your *Encounter* piece again.'

It was a very generous offer, but I was getting along rather better than he realized. The *Sunday Graphic* had bought the serialization rights of *Bang to Rights*, Secker & Warburg had given me a small advance to enable me to get started on my second book and I was earning £5 or £10 here and there from appearances on radio and television and occasional magazine articles.

On 16 October shortly after *Bang to Rights* was published, Ray wrote thanking me for the inscribed copy that I'd sent him. A second copy had been sent by Secker and he had given it to Jean Fracasse, an Australian lady who was working for him at the time. She'd enjoyed reading it but '... thought it faded a little at the end'. Ray's comment on this was: 'A real life story may easily lack the dramatic climax one has to contrive in fiction. The quality called suspense has to be in all fiction, although it may be got in various ways. The reader has to be made to want to know what is going to happen next. Life doesn't always give you this.' He mentioned how delighted he was with a Soho story that I had in the current issue of *Vogue*, then returned to my book. 'I think your description of the attitude of a man in prison, forbidden to be himself, deprived of his own personality on the surface and condemned to a continuous false façade – I think you do all this very well, and it is remarkable that you kept a sense of humour. Very much to be admired. There is good sound sense about the effect or non-effect of prisons in the book too ... Please let me know how things go with you ... No one who knows you would think of you as a natural wrongo, but a man can be driven to desperate things by persecution or hopelessness.' He was feeling pretty 'lost and worn out' at the time and I can't help wondering if that final gloomy observation was as much a reflection of his mood as it was a warning to me.

His last letter to me, dated 30 December 1958, was just fifty-nine words long: 'I was delighted to hear about your cocktail party and its success.' I'd thrown a book bash, in my Hampstead bedsitter, to launch *Bang to Rights*. Well over a hundred people turned up, some of them gate-crashers from the Soho underworld. Stephen Spender, Roger Senhouse and David Farrer from Secker, and the features editor of *Vogue* were absolutely enthralled to meet these bad-faced tearaways and were enchanted by their good manners. I wrote a piece about the party for the *Sunday Graphic* and sent Ray a cutting of it.

'I don't know how your book is going, but I hope it is going well,' he said and ended with what were to be his last words to me: 'What else am I to say – except that I wish you the best luck in the world for anything you do. Your friend, Ray.'

I could not have hoped for a more devoted and kindly mentor, if I'd chosen him myself and my gratitude is in no way diminished by the recent knowledge that he was steered in my direction by Natasha and Stephen Spender and did not therefore discover me for himself.

A Lasting Influence?

T. J. BINYON

It was about eleven o'clock in the morning, mid-October, with the sun not shining and a look of hard wet rain in the clearness of the foot-hills. I was wearing my powder-blue suit, with dark blue shirt, tie and display handkerchief, black brogues, black wool socks with dark blue clocks on them. I was neat, clean, shaved and sober, and I didn't care who knew it. I was everything the well-dressed private detective ought to be. I was calling on four million dollars.

The main hallway of the Sternwood place was two stories high. Over the entrance doors, which would have let in a troop of Indian elephants, there was a broad stained-glass panel showing a knight in dark armour rescuing a lady who was tied to a tree and didn't have any clothes on but some very long and convenient hair. The knight had pushed the vizor of his helmet back to be sociable, and he was fiddling with the knots on the ropes that tied the lady to the tree and not getting anywhere. I stood there and thought that if I lived in the house, I would sooner or later have to climb up there and help him. He didn't seem to be really trying.

In 1939 these witty, carefully detailed – the rain of the first sentence is falling at the end of the fourth chapter – opening paragraphs of *The Big Sleep* introduced Philip Marlowe to the reader. At the same time, through the use of language, through the attitude taken to the hero and to the milieu in which he was to move, they exemplified Chandler's intent 'to squeeze the last drop out of the medium', to use the formula of the detective story of his day to create 'something like literature out of it'.

In 'The Simple Art of Murder' Chandler, while praising Hammett's style, added that 'in his hands it had no overtones, left no echo, evoked no image beyond a distant hill'. The second paragraph of this extract, in which the figures on the stained-glass panel symbolically foreshadow Marlowe's progress throughout the novel, is an example of Chandler's attempt to remedy this, to bring together Hammett and Fitzgerald. This image seems to come off, but at other times Chandler is less successful. When Marlowe, at the end of *The High Window*, drives away after taking Merle Davis back to her parents and comments: 'I had a funny feeling as I saw the house disappear, as though I had written a poem and it was very good and I had lost it and would never remember it again', the sentiment strikes us as artificial – and as an imitation of Hemingway. But the effort, which on the whole succeeds more often than it fails, to give the language of his novels an extra, poetic resonance, is one of the distinguishing marks of Chandler's work.

The implicit identification of Marlowe in his powder-blue suit with the 'knight in dark armour' immediately creates an image of the hero which is spelt out in more detail in the famous passage in 'The Simple Art of Murder' which begins 'down these mean streets a man must go who is not himself mean, who is neither tarnished nor afraid'. Marlowe is a chivalrous man in an age when chivalry is dead; a man with a rigid and archaic code of honour. In *The High Window* Dr Carl Moss ironically calls him a 'shop-soiled Galahad'; Menendez, in *The Long Goodbye*, dismisses him scornfully as 'Tarzan on a big red scooter'. Whereas the functions of other detectives is to solve the mystery, nail the murderer and grab the loot. Marlowe's task, as Chandler wrote, is 'to protect the innocent, guard the helpless and destroy the wicked'. He is the one upright man in a corrupt society, a society epitomized throughout the novels by Bay City: 'Law is where you buy it in this town,' Marlowe tells Anne Riordan in *Farewell, My Lovely*. In a world where everything, including justice, is for sale, only Marlowe cannot be bought. Once again, the point has been made at the beginning of *The Big Sleep*, through the juxtaposition of the independent detective with the Sternwood wealth.

Since the appearance of *The Big Sleep* an immense number of novels, varying in quality from good to rubbish, have been written in what the English publishers of one example called 'the tough, hard-boiled vein of Dashiell Hammett and Raymond Chandler'. In most the central figure has been a private detective, but other favoured professions have been those of newspaperman, lawyer and insurance investigator. The locale has been most often California, with New York a short head behind, and Chicago trailing in third place. We have had female detectives: Marla Trent, heroine of Henry Kane's *The Private Eyeful* (1959), whose academic achievements – AB (Vassar), MA (NYU), PhD (Columbia) – are as implausible as her 38–23–38 figure; black detectives: Ernest Tidyman's John Shaft – slightly less unconvincing on celluloid than on the page – and J.F. Burke's Sam Kelly; and a homosexual insurance investigator: Dave Brandstetter of Medallion Life, who first appeared in Joseph Hansen's *Fadeout* (1970). Physical disability has not proved a handicap in the case of Michael Collins' Danny Fortune, who has only one arm, nor in that of Judson Philips' magazine columnist Peter Styles, who has only one leg.

Surprisingly enough, Chandler's influence on the vast majority of writers responsible for this flood of literature has been minimal, even non-existent. There is, of course, a superficial similarity between the Chandler novel and the typical private eye novel, since both employ the same basic formula. When Peter Chambers, Henry Kane's 'private richard', gives a mildly funny explanation of the conventions governing the hero's behaviour to a French art dealer in *Armchair in Hell* (1949), his summary is as applicable to Marlowe as to any other detective:

> He drinks, drinks more, and more; flirts with women, blondes mostly, who talk hard but act soft, then he drinks more, then, somewhere in the middle, he gets dreadfully beaten about, then he drinks more, then he says a few dirty words, then he stumbles around, punch-drunk-like, but he is very smart and he adds up a lot of two's and two's, and then the case gets solved.

Some stories show an occasional flash of wit, an occasional wisecrack or description, which raise a Chandlerian echo, but in general the only discernible connection is that their authors have taken to heart Chandler's advice on plotting formulated in his *Black Mask* days: 'When in doubt, have a man come through a door with a gun in his hand.'

There are, however, a few writers whose work shows more definite signs of being influenced by Chandler. Thomas B. Dewey's Mac, the best detective in Chicago, is, like Marlowe, a man with a social conscience. Dewey's novel *The Mean Streets* (1955) takes its title from Chandler's rhetorical invocation to his hero. In it Mac is employed by the Board of Education in a Mid-Western city to investigate the causes of a sudden rise in juvenile delinquency. Mac's sympathy for the young and exploited is undeniably Marlovian, but the violent methods he employs are closer to Spillane than to Chandler, while the analysis of social problems is more than simplistic. Behind the wave of juvenile crime lies an organization headed by the mysterious 'Mr Smith', revealed by Mac to be Cameron, an attorney and 'prominent civic leader'. His death, it is implied, will restore peace to the town.

Harold Q. Masur's early novels about a New York lawyer, Scott Jordan, are brighter and wittier than most, but otherwise are indistinguishable from the common run. The later books, however, are better plotted, more subtle, and Scott Jordan begins to take on Marlowe's knight-errant role. 'If I see a stranger in jeopardy, I ride to the rescue,' he remarks. The style changes, in a seemingly conscious effort to obtain Chandler's effects. 'I had an odd sense of unreality, as if this colloquy were taking place between faceless people in a bad dream' is an image from *The Legacy Lenders* (1967); a very different tone from that of *Suddenly a Corpse* (1949), in which a character is described as being as 'alert as a squirrel and tougher than yesterday's egg-stains'. At the same time Masur introduces into his work an increasing number of reflections on the progress of urban civilization and the consequences of technological innovation: themes which, linked or co-existing with the theme of corruption, become characteristic of the social comment in the post-Chandlerian novel.

William Campbell Gault is obviously a great admirer of Chandler, as are his characters. In *Don't Cry For Me* (1952) the hero, Pete Worden, tells the police lieutenant that the case would never have been solved, if he, Worden, had not been 'sensitive, intuitive and a reader of Chandler'.

Gault's most successful detective is Brock 'the Rock' Callahan, a former guard on the Los Angeles Rams, who tends, in moments of depression, to compare himself unfavourably with Philip Marlowe. He makes his appearance in *Ring Round Rosa* (1955) which contains an apology for police behaviour: 'They're underpaid and overworked. They deal with rapists and murderers, with child molesters and wife-beaters. All day long they meet arrogance and deceit and hate ...' which is very similar in mood to the slightly unreal long set speech delivered by Christy French to Marlowe in *The Little Sister*. Two other good Callahan novels are *The Convertible Hearse* (1957), in which the used-car trade becomes an ironic symbol for the American way of life, and *Day of the Ram* (1956), about the murder of a brilliant young quarterback who has just made a miraculous debut for the Rams. The football game is excellently described. In this novel Callahan is beaten up in a Santa Monica bookie joint and then arrested; there follows a dialogue between him and the chief of the Santa Monica police which is comprehensible only to Chandler readers:

'Evidently you don't know our little town.'
'I read about it,' I said, 'but the writer called it Bay City.'

Though these authors have obviously been influenced by Chandler, the influence has not been a deep and significant one, as it has been with Ross Macdonald, who has adapted and developed his predecessor's material in an extremely interesting way.

The comparison between Chandler and Macdonald is one which has been made many times. Like Chandler, Macdonald has succeeded in turning the conventional detective story formula into a novel in its own right; indeed, the *New York Times* has called him 'one of the best American novelists now operating'. Whether his Lew Archer stories are better than Chandler's work is a question that must be resolved by individual taste. Barzun and Taylor, in their *Catalogue of Crime* (1971), consider that in Macdonald 'the California scene is often better (because less outré) than Chandler's and the psychology and social observation are more original and penetrating.' Julian Symons, in *Bloody Murder* (1972), thinks that Macdonald could have been 'not merely the lineal successor to Hammett and Chandler, but even their superior', but that 'the development that one hoped for has not quite taken place'. It must be said that though the plots are often hideously complex, the best – in, for instance, *The Ivory Grin* (1952) or *The Zebra-Striped Hearse* (1962) – are more satisfying than Chandler's, though one or two – *The Wycherley Woman* (1961) and *The Chill* (1963) are marred by improbabilities which one does not meet in Chandler.

Macdonald's language strives hard for effect; he consciously avoids the easy relaxation which Chandler shows in narrative passages; his pages are a constant succession of striking images. At its best his style can convey violence and frenzy with impressive force, or, as in the last pages of *The Drowning Pool* (1950), impart almost lyrical overtones to a scene – here a daughter's recognition of her father. In his latest novels, however, his images often seem over-explicit or over-emphasized, as in this example from *Sleeping Beauty* (1973): 'They were like astronauts artificially sustained on an alien planet, careful but contemptuous of the unfriendly environment and its unlikely inhabitants'; or the description of an unhappily married couple playing tennis with which *The Blue Hammer* (1976) opens: 'Something about the trapped intensity of their game reminded me of prisoners in an exercise yard.'

There is much less humour in Macdonald than in Chandler; this partly reflects the fact that the wisecrack is now out-of-date, but Archer is also too serious to be as spontaneously funny as Marlowe can be on occasion. He is a less idealized figure than Marlowe. Though the title *Sleeping Beauty* has a hint of the knight image, other references to it are ironic: 'I thought I was rescuing a maiden from a tower. Fall guys usually do, I guess,' or analytic: 'He had the knight-errant look in his eyes, that Galahad fluorescence compounded of idealism and hysteria and sublimated sex.'

Archer is a more complicated character than Marlowe; more down-to-earth; more likely – though this probably only reflects changing attitudes – to go to bed with a woman during the course of a novel; more moralistic, in his attempts to force other characters to recognize duties and obligations – a tendency which affects Marlowe only in later life; and yet at the same time he is much more prone to self-disgust, when his profession and his feelings are at odds: 'I hated to lie when the human element cut across my work,' he comments.

He is more cultured than Marlowe: he only pretends not to recognize Proust's name, and when he calls someone 'a sociopath with schizoid tendencies', he knows what he means. But his habit of referring to the *Gestalt* of a case is an annoying one. He is perhaps a more credible character than Marlowe, better realized, in novelistic terms, but not quite as attractive.

As in Chandler, corruption and greed pervade the Californian atmosphere, but the author's indignation is aroused primarily by their consequences for the environment. Man-made disasters play an important thematic part in two novels – a forest fire in *The Underground Man* (1971), and an oil-spill from an offshore well in *Sleeping Beauty*. This passage from *The Drowning Pool* sums up his views:

> I turned on my back and floated, looking up at the sky, nothing around me but cool clear Pacific, nothing in my eyes but long blue space. It was as close as I ever got to cleanliness and freedom, as far as I ever got from all the people. They had jerrybuilt the beaches from San Diego to the Golden Gate, bulldozed super-highways through the mountains, cut down a thousand years of redwood growth, and built an urban wilderness in the desert. They couldn't touch the ocean. They poured their sewage into it, but it couldn't be tainted.

While organized crime and the professional criminal are a constant element in Chandler's works, in Macdonald they become less and less important, vanishing almost completely in his latest novels. Instead, in a peculiar throwback to an earlier type of detective story, almost to a Victorian novel, Lew Archer becomes involved in complex webs of family relationships, uncovers concealed identities, restores lost parents to children, investigates crimes with roots lying deep in the past. Whereas Marlowe represents an ethical ideal, Archer has a less imposing role: he acts as mediator between uncomprehending parents and their incomprehensible children; he is a man with a mission to protect the erring

177

young from the consequences of their parents' guilt, and from their own foolishness and immaturity. Each novel contains one or more adolescents whom he befriends, helps, and ends by taking as surrogates for the children he does not have. 'I was old enough to be his father, with no son of my own,' he says of Alex Kincaid in *The Chill*; and of Peter Jamieson in *Black Money* (1965): 'I'd fathered an imaginary son, a poor fat foolish son who ate his sorrow instead of drinking it'; and, in *The Blue Hammer*: 'I turned off the light and fell back into sleep, breathing in unison with my pseudo-son.'

John D. MacDonald's series of novels about Travis McGee have few, if any pretensions to be treated as serious literature. Nevertheless, they are exciting and entertaining on their own level, and McGee is certainly a further development of the Marlovian hero.

In *The Deep Blue Goodbye* (1964), the first of the series, McGee describes himself as 'that peace-seeker, iconoclast, disbeliever, argufier, that knuckly scar-tissued reject from a structured society'. Like Marlowe he is an individualist, a romantic idealist. He sees himself as a knight-errant, and the plot of each novel consists, in essence, of the rescue of a beleaguered maiden from an evil dragon. But, unlike Marlowe, he knows that he is out-of-date, and references to his self-imposed role are invariably mocking: 'No matter what the bastards did, McGee would keep trying. He would keep on clattering in there, banging the rusty armour, spurring the spavined old steed, waving the mad crooked lance.' And, unlike Archer, he never feels his methods and his ethics to be in conflict. He has a rigid code of honour, but it is confined to his private life; his world is black and white, divided into enemies, to whom the code does not apply, and friends, to whom it does.

The standard formula of the detective novel has a centripetal plot: though the hero may drive round a city, visit its suburbs, or travel to other towns, he invariably returns more or less to his starting point. *The Big Sleep*, a more formal example than most, begins and ends in the Sternwood mansion. John D. MacDonald, however, tends to employ the thriller formula, that of a chase, which is centrifugal. Though most of his novels begin in Florida, where McGee lives aboard his houseboat *The Busted Flush* in Bahia Mar, Lauderdale, they can take him to New York, Chicago, Hollywood, Mexico or even – in *The Turquoise Lament* (1973) – Pago-Pago.

The novels are disfigured by a broad and embarrassing streak of sentimentality. This emerges particularly in McGee's relationships with women, which usually begin with his belief that bed is a sure cure for everything from gunshot wounds to agoraphobia. Sentimentality pervades the language as well. When, in *A Tan and Sandy Silence* (1972), McGee formulates his philosophy:

> Up with life. Stamp out all small and large indignities. Leave everyone alone to make it without pressure. Down with hurting. Lower the standard of living. Do without plastics. Smash the servo-mechanisms. Stop grabbing. Snuff the breeze and hug the kids. Love all love. Hate all hate ...

one might admire the sentiments, but cringe at their expression.

But this quality is generally redeemed by excellent intrigue and sharp observation. The novels continue Chandler's tradition of social comment, but have different targets. MacDonald makes interesting and acerbic comments on the corruptions of big business, which he connects with the insipid, bland and banal homogeneity of contemporary America, and, like Ross Macdonald, with the pollution of the environment. But his comments are often more acute than the latter's, being more knowledgeable and less generalized. These quotations from *The Dreadful Lemon Sky* (1975) and *The Scarlet Ruse* (1973) give the flavour:

> There had been a little town on the bay shore, a few hundred people, a sleepy downtown with live oaks and Spanish moss. Then International Amalgamated Development had moved in, bought a couple of thousand acres, and put in shopping centres, town houses, condominiums and rental apartments just south of town. Next had arrived Consolidated Construction Enterprises and done the same thing north of town. Smaller operators had done the same things on a smaller scale west of town. When downtown decayed, the town fathers widened the streets and cut down the shade trees in an attempt to look just like a shopping centre. It didn't work. It never does. This was instant Florida, tacky and stifling and full of ugly and spurious energies. They had every chain food-service outfit known to man, interspersed with used-car lots and furniture stores.

> She might be impressed were I to cruise into Tallabea Bay and describe to her the one and a half billion tons of untreated wastes from Constitution-Carbo Combine which put a two-foot coat on the bottom of the bay. Or we could take a tour up into the mountains

179

to watch how the trade winds carry the bourbon-coloured stink of petro-chemical stacks through the passes all the way to Mayaguez, ninety miles from the refineries. While in the hills, we could check and see if Leviathan Copper and Landmark Super Steels have started to strip-mine the seven square green tropic miles of high land which they covet.

The qualities of Chandler's novels were recognized in England earlier than in America, and they rapidly – especially in association with Humphrey Bogart's portrayal of Marlowe in the Warner Brothers 1946 version of *The Big Sleep* – became the objects of a cult, to which Neville Smith's screenplay for the film *Gumshoe* (1971) paid an affectionate parodic tribute.

Nevertheless, Chandler seems to have had very little direct effect on English writers. That the conventions of the English crime novel should have become looser, that it should have become seamier, tougher and more violent in recent years, can be attributed not specifically to Chandler, but to the influence of the whole school of American fiction. Occasionally a closer connection can be discovered. Julian Symons is undoubtedly right when he calls the Chief Detective-Inspector and Sergeant in John Bingham's *My Name is Michael Sibley* (1952) 'polite English versions of Chandler's policemen', while the description of police methods in his own *The Progress of a Crime* (1960) seems informed by the same source.

The difficulty writers have faced has been that of transposing the private detective, his methods and his milieu to an English scene while retaining some semblance of credibility. It has often been done, on the pulp level, but Clark Smith is the only writer worthy of consideration to have attempted it. The effort, though valiant, seems misconceived and unsuccessful. His hero Nicky Mahoun is, like the author himself, an accountant. In *The Speaking Eye* (1955) he investigates the crooked accounts of a small engineering firm in Scotland; in *The Deadly Reaper* (1956) he uncovers a drug-smuggling ring in the West of England.

Chandlerian echoes are everywhere in these novels. While Mahoun is interviewing Melville Strype, a fellow chartered accountant: 'He put his little finger in his ear, moved it round a couple of times, then took it out and stared at it.' Compare Chandler's treatment of the same nasty habit in the meeting between Marlowe and the numismatist Elisha Morningstar (*The High Window*): 'He stuck his little finger in his ear and worked it round and brought it out with a little dark wax on it. He wiped it off casually on his coat.'

Occasionally Smith achieves something like the Chandler effect: 'An idea nudged me, then looked away.' And: 'It was a man's room and you weren't welcome in it unless you smoked a pipe, wore a regimental tie and read the Tatler before breakfast.' More often than not, however, the result is a hilarious blend of American and English slang and attitudes:

'I really don't like your manner,' he said.
'Sickening, isn't it?' I said. 'I'm jolly disgusted with it myself.'

One scene in *The Deadly Reaper* – the ritual confrontation between hero and chauffeur or stud (Marlowe with the Grayles' chauffeur in *Farewell, My Lovely*; with Vannier in *The High Window*; with Chris Lavery in *The Lady In The Lake*) – deserves to be quoted in full:

'Looking for something, chum?' he said. He came round the car so that I could see how big and strong he was.
'Just looking the place over,' I said.
'Some other time, chum – when you've got an appointment.'
I looked at the muscles on his chest as he squeezed the sponge he was holding. He squeezed it more than he needed to.
'It's courtesy to ask,' I said.
He came towards me, arching his chest menacingly. 'I don't like the lip,' he said.
I put my hands in my pockets in case I felt like swiping him. 'You're making a mistake, superboy. I'll play tell-tales with your boss.'
The muscles in his arms jumped as he clenched his hands. 'You'll be spitting teeth if you don't knock off, chum.'
'Aw,' I said. 'Isn't that tough. Comrade Hellmet sitting in there all ready for me; and me too busy spitting teeth to talk to him.'

Smith's third, and apparently last novel, *The Case of Torches* (1957) drops the fake Americanisms, the excessive violence and the inept love-making of the first two, but retains a tight plot and sound financial detail.

Though Ross Macdonald and John D. MacDonald are still writing about Lew Archer and Travis McGee, their heroes are getting older; the knight-errant, never a very plausible figure, has become a complete anachronism; and it is now beginning to seem less and less possible to create a new hero in Marlowe's mould. But the temptation is there, and several American writers have succumbed to it recently.

Peter Israel, in two novels written in a bright, sub-Chandlerian style – *Hush Money* (1975) and *The French Kiss* (1976) – has created an anti-Marlowe. His hero, B.F. Cage, begins by explicitly dissociating himself from Chandler's and Macdonald's characters: he has no ethics, he says; he is in the business only for money. The concept is superficially ingenious, but it is not taken far enough. A genuinely evil Marlowe might have worked, but a Marlowe who merely shares the greed and acquisitiveness of the society which surrounds him is without interest.

Another solution to the problem has been found by Andrew Bergman, who puts Jack LeVine, his balding, Jewish private eye back into the age of Chandler. In *The Big Kiss-Off of 1944* (1974) LeVine becomes involved in Dewey's campaign against Roosevelt; in *Hollywood and LeVine* (1975) – a better book – he investigates a murder on Marlowe's home territory and meets Humphrey Bogart and a young US Congressman called Richard Nixon. Bergman's parody can be witty and inventive, but it is parody, and hence a dead end.

Robert B. Parker's approach to the problem is the boldest: he simply ignores it. His hero, Spenser, a Boston private detective who has so far appeared in *The Godwulf Manuscript* (1973), *God Save the Child* (1974) and *Mortal Stakes* (1975), is an affectionate imitation of Marlowe.

Marlowe was originally called Mallory (in 'Blackmailers Don't Shoot'), a name with echoes of the Round Table; Spenser evokes the Knights of the Faerie Queene and, just in case we miss the reference, he tells us: 'It's with an *s*, not a *c*. Like the English poet.' Marlowe has an affair with Linda Loring; Spenser is having one with Brenda Loring. Marlowe's business card had a tommy gun in the corner; Spenser's has crossed daggers. Marlowe was fired from the District Attorney's office for insubordination; Spenser was fired from the police for insubordination.

Parker's books are quite entertaining as pastiche, but they are no more than this. The prose lacks the density and texture of Chandler, and the ethic is spelt, rather than acted out. In *Mortal Stakes* Spenser's girl tries to work out over a meal why he is distressed after killing two hoodlums with a shotgun at pointblank range:

'Two moral imperatives in your system are never to allow innocents to be victimized and never to kill people except involuntarily. Perhaps

the words aren't quite the right ones, but that's the idea, isn't it?'
I nodded.

'And,' she said, 'this time you couldn't obey both those imperatives. You had to violate one.'

I nodded again.

'I understand,' she said.

We ate for a bit in silence.

'I can't make it better,' she said.

'No,' I said. 'You can't.'

We ate the rest of the entrée in silence.

The waiter brought coffee. 'You will live a little diminished, won't you?' she said.

This scene is unintentionally funny, and its artificiality can be seen by contrast with Chandler's understated treatment of the same moral problem in *The Big Sleep*: the conversation between Mona Mars and Marlowe, after he has shot Lash Camino:

'I – I was afraid you'd come back.'

I said: 'We had a date. I told you it was all arranged.' I began to laugh like a loon.

Then she was bending down over him, touching him. And after a little while she stood up with a small key on a thin chain.

She said bitterly: 'Did you have to kill him?'

I stopped laughing as suddenly as I had started. She went behind me and unlocked the handcuffs.

'Yes,' she said softly. 'I suppose you did.'

The fact that pastiche, imitation and parody have taken over implies that the Chandler epoch in detective fiction is now coming to an end: it is difficult to see in what way the tradition might be further seriously developed. At the same time, however, Chandler's work still seems to be exerting an influence, if a less direct one, in other spheres: on the adventure story and the spy novel. The tough, sardonic, slightly battered heroes of Gavin Lyall, for instance, are direct descendants of Philip Marlowe, while the spies of Le Carré and Deighton, in their radical distrust of all authority, embody, if in a very different way, the revolt against a corrupt society that Marlowe represented.

Bibliography

BOOKS

The Big Sleep Knopf, New York, 1939; Hamish Hamilton, London, 1939

Farewell, My Lovely Knopf, New York, 1940; Hamish Hamilton, London, 1940

The High Window Knopf, New York, 1942; Hamish Hamilton, London, 1943

The Lady in the Lake Knopf, New York, 1943; Hamish Hamilton, London, 1944

The Little Sister Hamish Hamilton, London, 1949; Houghton Mifflin, Boston, 1949

The Long Goodbye Hamish Hamilton, London, 1953; Houghton Mifflin, Boston, 1954

Playback Hamish Hamilton, London, 1958; Houghton Mifflin, Boston, 1958

STORIES

'Blackmailers Don't Shoot', *Black Mask*, December 1933

'Smart-Aleck Kill', *Black Mask*, July 1934

'Finger Man', *Black Mask*, October 1934

'Killer in the Rain', *Black Mask*, January 1935

'Nevada Gas', *Black Mask*, June 1935

'Spanish Blood', *Black Mask*, November 1935

'Guns at Cyrano's', *Black Mask*, January 1936

'The Man Who Liked Dogs', *Black Mask*, March 1936

'Noon Street Nemesis' (republished as 'Pick-Up on Noon Street'), *Detective Fiction Weekly*, 30 May 1936

'Goldfish', *Black Mask*, June 1936

'The Curtain', *Black Mask*, September 1936

'Try the Girl', *Black Mask*, January 1937

'Mandarin's Jade', *Dime Detective Magazine*, November 1937

'Red Wind', *Dime Detective Magazine*, January 1938

'The King in Yellow', *Dime Detective Magazine*, March 1938

'Bay City Blues', *Dime Detective Magazine*, January 1938

'The Lady in the Lake', *Dime Detective Magazine*, January 1939

'Pearls Are a Nuisance', *Dime Detective Magazine*, April 1939

'Trouble is My Business', *Dime Detective Magazine*, August 1939

'I'll be Waiting', *Saturday Evening Post*, 14 October 1939

'The Bronze Door', *Unknown*, November 1939

'No Crime in the Mountains', *Detective Story*, September 1941

'Professor Bingo's Snuff', *Park East*, June–August 1951; *Go*, June–July 1951

'Marlowe Takes on the Syndicate', *Daily Mail*, 6–10 April 1959, also. published as 'Wrong Pidgeon', *Manhunt*, February 1961. Reprinted as 'The Pencil'

ARTICLES

'The Simple Art of Murder', *Atlantic Monthly*, December 1944

'Writers in Hollywood', *Atlantic Monthly*, November 1945

'Oscar Night in Hollywood', *Atlantic Monthly*, March 1948

'The Simple Art of Murder', *Saturday Review of Literature*, 15 April 1950

'Ten Per Cent of Your Life', *Atlantic Monthly*, February 1952

The Contributors

JACQUES BARZUN is one of America's foremost men of letters. He was Provost and Professor at Columbia University, NY, for many years and is at present literary adviser to Charles Scribner's Sons. His books include *The House of Intellect, Berlioz and the Romantic Century, Classic, Romantic and Modern* and *The American University*.

T.J. BINYON teaches Russian literature at Oxford. He reviews crime fiction regularly for the *Times Literary Supplement*.

RUSSELL DAVIES, after periods spent in academic research and television review, became a freelance journalist and illustrator. He is now film critic of *The Observer*.

PHILIP FRENCH has worked for many years in BBC Radio, specializing in programmes on the Arts and American affairs. He contributes regularly to *The Observer, The Times, New Statesman, TLS*, and *Sight and Sound*. His books include *The Movie Moguls* and *Westerns*, and his essays have been reprinted in numerous anthologies in Britain and America.

MICHAEL GILBERT has been a prolific author of crime novels and short stories since 1947. He is a partner in a Lincoln's Inn firm of solicitors and acted as Chandler's English solicitor. He is editor of the series 'Classics of Adventure and Detection' published by Hodder & Stoughton.

PATRICIA HIGHSMITH was born in Texas and educated in New York. Her first novel, *Stranger on a Train* was filmed by Alfred Hitchcock with a script by Raymond Chandler. Her other novels include *The Talented Mr Ripley*, *This Sweet Sickness*, *Ripley's Game* and, most recently, *Edith's Diary*. She now lives in France.

ERIC HOMBERGER was educated at the University of California, Chicago and Cambridge. He is now Lecturer in American Literature at the University of East Anglia. He has edited *Ezra Pound: The Critical Heritage* (1972) and is the author of *The Art of the Real: Poetry in England and America since 1939* (1977).

JOHN HOUSEMAN, who has produced many Hollywood films, is also a distinguished writer (*Runthrough*, 1972) and actor. He is at present Artistic Director of The Acting Company, New York.

CLIVE JAMES was educated at Sydney University and Cambridge. As well as being the regular television critic for *The Observer* he is the author of *The Metropolitan Critic*, *Fan-Mail*, *Visions Before Midnight* and three mock epic poems – 'Peregrine Prykke's Pilgrimage', 'The Fate of Felicity Fark', and 'Britannia Bright's Bewilderment'.

MICHAEL MASON is a lecturer at University College, London. He has written a book on James Joyce and is at present working on a novel.

FRANK NORMAN was brought up in the care of Dr Barnardo's Homes, after which he became an habitué of sleazy gambling dens, clip joints and small urn-steaming cafés of a thriving Soho underworld, and was continually in trouble with the police, serving several prison sentences. He began writing in 1957 and has published thirteen books, which include *Banana Boy*, *Stand on Me*, *Much Ado About Nuffink* and *Down and Out in High Society*. He is the author of the musical *Fings Ain't Wot They Used T'Be* and three other plays.

DILYS POWELL was for nearly forty years film critic of the *Sunday Times*. Author of several books about Greece, she has had a long connection with the world of writers; and she and her husband, the late Leonard Russell, who was Literary Editor of the *Sunday Times*, were among the first serious admirers of Raymond Chandler.

NATASHA SPENDER had a successful career as a concert pianist under the name Natasha Litvin. She is now a lecturer and research writer on the experimental psychology of music.

JULIAN SYMONS was recently elected President of the Detection Club of Great Britain in succession to Agatha Christie. He is the author of a history of crime writing, *Bloody Murder*, of criminological studies and biographies, and of numerous crime novels, among them *The Colour of Murder*, winner of the Crime Writers' Association prize for 1953. He has also established a distinguished reputation as a biographer, military historian and literary critic.

BILLY WILDER went to Hollywood from Austria in the early 1930s and became one of its most successful and best-known directors. Apart from *Double Indemnity*, which he directed and co-scripted with Chandler, his films include *The Lost Weekend* (1945), *Sunset Boulevard* (1950), *The Seven-Year Itch* (1955), *Some Like It Hot* (1959) and *The Apartment* (1960).

Acknowledgements

The editor and publishers are grateful to the following people and organizations for their help and permission to reproduce copyright material:

For illustrations from: the University of California, Los Angeles, Department of Special Collections pages 1, 2 (*above*), 3 (*above*), 6 (*above*) and 8 (*left*); Hamish Hamilton page 2 (*below*); Kobal Collection pages 3 (*below*), 16 (*above*), 18 (*below*), 20 (*above and below left*), 21 (*above and below right*), 22 (*above left and below right*), 23 (*left above and below, and right below*); Associated Press page 4 (*above*); Natasha Spender pages 5 (*below right*), 7 (*above and below*), 8 (*right*); Dilys Powell page 5 (*above left*); Mark Gerson page 5 (*above right*); Frank Norman page 5 (*below left*); Topix page 6 (*below*); BBC Television page 20 (*bottom left*); National Film Archive, London, all other photographs.

Helga Greene and Hamish Hamilton Ltd for quotations from Raymond Chandler's published work and correspondence.

Raymond Chandler Speaking, edited by Dorothy Gardiner and Kathrine Sorley Walker, Hamish Hamilton, London; Houghton Mifflin, Boston.

The Life of Raymond Chandler, by Frank MacShane, Jonathan Cape, London; Dutton, New York.

The Notebooks of Raymond Chandler and English Summer, edited by Frank MacShane. Weidenfeld, London; Ecco Press, New York.

Down These Mean Streets A Man Must Go, by Philip Durham, University of North Carolina Press.

Raymond Chandler, A Checklist, by Matthew J. Bruccoli, Kent State University Press.

Chandler Before Marlowe, edited by Matthew J. Bruccoli, University of South Carolina Press.